HEATHER L. COLE

BUSINESS
INTELLIGENCE
BULL'S-EYE

THE EXECUTIVE'S GUIDE

CONQUER YOUR MARKET AND
TRANSFORM YOUR ORGANIZATION
WITH DATA AND ANALYTICS

FREE - Bonus Resources

This book references tools you can use to transform your company to become data and analytics driven. The first step is to identify your problem areas with the Business Intelligence Action Assessment Indicator.

Sign up today to receive access to the complete Business Intelligence Bull's-eye Executive Guide resource library.

GET IT NOW at www.Heatherized.com/BookBonus

Printed in the United States of America.

ISBN (Print)
978-1-7320014-0-4

First Edition

Dedicated to my clients, team and friends
who inspire me on a daily basis and validate that we
can improve the world by leveraging data and analytics.

Table of Contents

Introduction to Business Intelligence Bull's-eye   1

CHAPTER 1
Business Intelligence Challenge   5

CHAPTER 2
Are You an Analytic Leader?   11

CHAPTER 3
Learning the Basics   29

CHAPTER 4
Executive Buy-In   51

CHAPTER 5
Building Your Special Forces   79

CHAPTER 6
All In   97

CHAPTER 7
Crazy Ideas Welcome!   103

CHAPTER 8
Lessons Learned   125

Let's Continue Working Together   131

Other Programs and Offerings by Heatherized: 133

About the Author   135

Acknowledgements   137

Endnotes   139

FREE BONUS

Because I hate to see organizations struggle with business intelligence, I have created a membership website that has additional resources and tools from this book. The great news is that access to the site is completely free. All I ask is for your contact information so I can send you updates and keep in touch. Log in today at www.Heatherized.com/BookBonus.

Here is what you'll receive:

- Downloadable forms like the BI Action Assessment Indicator, Core Values worksheet, and questionnaires
- Sample job description for attracting BI superstars
- Videos to improve communication and provide time-saving methods
- Personal invites to exclusive events
- And more!

Sign up today at www.Heatherized.com/BookBonus.

Introduction to Business Intelligence Bull's-eye

Congratulations! You have taken the first step to becoming an analytic leader. This book represents nearly 20 years of hard work, experience, personal development programs, and insights from my amazing customers. Maybe you're one of them! I wanted to take a moment to share some thoughts with you about what to expect from this book.

I've written this for executives of companies to learn how to support the business intelligence professionals and data scientists who are struggling to realize the full potential of tools that deliver data and analytics.

I've read hundreds of books on business intelligence, data warehousing, analytics, and leadership. Many are fabulous for technically astute people but would confuse the executive whose last exposure to statistics was 30 years ago in college. My goal in this book is to empower the executives that want to lead their organizations to dominate their markets during the data and analytics revolution. I want executives to feel comfortable and understand the basics. Every executive must understand that funding and sponsoring business intelligence initiatives is not enough. Executive engagement is required. Most organizations are setting the hard-working data scientists and IT teams up for failure by not communicating the strategic direction of the organization or the plan on how to get there. They expect business intelligence teams to magically read their minds.

Lack of communication is the root of business intelligence failures. This book introduces you to pragmatic methods that you can implement in your organization immediately.

This book is not a technical manual. It's written as a parable and designed to share my ideas and the Business Intelligence Bull's-eye methodology with you. It is intended to help you succeed at business intelligence and leverage data to better serve your customers, employees, and the world. It is a book for implementers. If you aren't committed to transformation, committed to trying something new, committed to investing your time, then don't bother reading this book. Dabblers don't deliver!

In this book, the characters will utilize a number of templates, forms, and other tools that I use with my clients. I have made many of these tools available to you for free at www.heatherized.com/bookbonus.

This book wasn't intended to be a *NY Times* #1 Bestseller. It's designed to start a conversation with you, give us a chance to get to know each other better, develop trust and a bond, and, ultimately, help us decide if we will work together someday.

This book is packed with creative ideas, but it is not a complete step-by-step book. My intention and the purpose of this book is to introduce you the most powerful ways to succeed on the journey to becoming a data and analytics driven organization. The methods I use are very simplistic, and that's the beauty of it. This book does not cover all of it, but I do have a how-to system available that includes everything you need to execute what you read in these pages.

My goal is to empower every company, regardless of size, or industry to leverage data, analytics and artificial intelligence.

The best way to start a relationship with me is to visit www .Heatherized.com/BookBonus and sign up for the supplemental tools for this book. Please share your ideas and thoughts as you use the tools. I'm looking forward to getting to know you better!

Sincerely,
Heather L. Cole
Tampa, Florida and Breckenridge, Colorado

PS: I wrote and edited this book myself. I'll be the first to admit my first language is numbers, but my team told me writing it in binary or hexadecimal wasn't allowed. There are probably some spelling, grammatical, and layout errors. If you find one, will you do me a favor and tell me what you find by sending me an email at hcole@heatherized.com? Just note the page number, sentence, and mistake, and I'll fix it right away. Thank you for your help.

I'm all about results, implementation, and speed and chose to provide you with tools that give you rapid results over perfection and procrastination. Money loves speed, and time kills opportunities.

PPS: If you love this book, will you please post a review on Amazon at www.heatherized.com/BIBullseyeReview. If you DON'T like it, send me an email, tell me why, and I'll give you your money back, ok? My direct email is hcole@heatherized.com. Please be kind; my mom reads the reviews. This is my first book and a 15-year dream come to reality.

CHAPTER 1

Business Intelligence Challenge

*"All you need is a plan, the road map,
and the courage to press on to your destination."*

–Earl Nightingale

It was a bright, sunny day as I walked into the office. I could feel the tension in the air. I thought maybe my five-mile run in the morning would help relieve the pressure, but I was wrong. My assistant, Sarah, greeted me with a hot cup of coffee and said, "Another day in the trenches. Chris and Bob are in the Chicago conference room. Sounds a little heated. You might want to check in on them."

"Thanks Sarah. Let me get my ducks in a row, and I will find out what's going on."

After booting up my computer and checking for any urgent emails, I approached the Chicago conference room. I heard Bob stating, "Chris, you gotta work with me on this!"

As I opened the door, both men looked up at me. "James, you're just in time. Maybe you can help settle our disagreement. Chris and I have been exploring ideas on how we can better utilize data. As you know, we were challenged to get basic business intelligence rolled out and, more importantly, to get end-users to actually use the solution. Chris thinks that if we let the departments choose their own solutions, then it could free IT up to focus on urgent matters," said Bob McFarland, the Chief Information Officer, with a frustrated look on his face.

Bob McFarland is an average-size man with balding hair and bright blue eyes. He had been with Playfair Distributing for about five years and has great ideas. He is forward-thinking and manages his team well but has been struggling to find the time and resources to deliver successful business intelligence. Bob often had disagreements with Chris Hayward, the Chief Financial Officer, because Bob felt he was not getting the funding necessary to help transform the company into the digital age.

Chris, on the other hand, felt that Bob wasn't delivering. Chris Hayward was an athletically-built man in his late 40s. Not your typical financial executive. His background included a MBA from the University of Chicago and an undergraduate degree in computer science. Chris was a more technologically advanced CFO. Chris's can-do attitude and technology background was why we heavily recruited him to join Playfair Distributing. I knew when we hired him that Bob may feel a little intimidated by Chris; however, I believed Bob would step up to the challenge. Chris had asked many times for a financial dashboard, but every time the IT team delivered a dashboard, it did not meet the finance department's needs. Chris expressed to me he wanted to purchase a new cloud-based software that would allow his finance team to be self-sufficient and generate the reports and analysis they needed without relying on IT.

"James, you know my team is handcuffed. Every time we want to do analysis, we have to go to IT to get access to the data, resulting in huge delays. If we can buy a solution designed for finance, we wouldn't have to burden the IT department. This would allow Bob's team to focus on more innovative areas that could change our future." Chris was clearly positioning. "I think we all want the same thing here, don't you?" Chris said this while placing his hands on his hips.

"Yes, I think we do want the same thing!" I said. "You guys know my hot buttons: increase market share, increase efficiencies, increase profits, and become one of the most innovative distribution companies in the market. But we are not going to get there if we don't agree on how to get there. Maybe we need to take a step back before we spend more money. I think we need to understand what we own and what we need it to do. In my mind, there's no reason the software we have cannot do the job."

"You know the board recently inquired if we were thinking about the future and artificial intelligence, but candidly, I'm struggling. We've spent hundreds of thousands of dollars on high-paid consultants and expensive software, not to mention our own team's time trying to deliver business intelligence solutions, but for some reason, we are just not as successful as I'd hoped. Bob, don't take this the wrong way. I know your guys are trying hard, but for some reason, it seems to take a lot longer for your team to deliver, and now, we need to think about leveraging artificial intelligence," I said, shaking my head. "What can we do to help your guys be successful?"

"There isn't just one thing," Bob explained. "We have a number of challenges. The data is not as clean as we needed. That's why keep asking for funding for a data warehouse. We need to create data governance policies and have people adhere to them. My team is great technologically, but it needs more engagement from the end users. There appears to be a huge disconnect. It's almost as if end users don't want better tools. We build solutions, and the end users say they prefer to use the reports they are used to using. We provide training programs, but end users refuse to attend. I'm just as frustrated as you guys. I am open to ideas, but we are doing the best we can."

"I'm afraid that if we don't do something quickly, our competitors will beat us in digital transformation, and that could be a massive hit to our bottom line," expressed Chris, the CFO. "I was on a webinar the other day that explored the role of predictive analytics in the office of finance, and I strongly feel that we need to get there and get there fast."

"I agree!" I said. "I read a KPMG report that said that according to surveyed CEOs, data and analytics would be one of their top three investment priorities over the next three years. But all the talk about artificial intelligence, predictive analytics, big data, data warehousing, prescriptive analytics, and business intelligence makes my head spin. I don't even know where to start. And Bob, I know you're very capable, but you are already stretched so thin as it is. I love that you guys are discussing this, but my gut tells me that additional systems are not the answer. Can't the business intelligence tools we bought last year deliver what you want, Chris? You were involved in that selection process."

"Yes, our business intelligence tools will deliver what Chris's team needs. But they want to do everything themselves, which I am not opposed to in the long run. However, they need to be trained. The problem is, I don't feel comfortable training them until the data is clean and in a format that they will understand. If we give them access to the data and tools now, they will end up making decisions based on bad data," said Bob.

My phone buzzed. I looked down and noticed I had an 8:30 meeting I needed to attend. "We will not resolve this today. I suggest we schedule some time and do some brainstorming in the next week. Let's all think about this and talk to our teams. Bob can you please schedule a strategy session."

As I turned to the door, I looked back and said, "You guys know I believe in you, right? Together, we will figure this out. I'm just not sure how yet."

As I left the room, my mind was spinning. How can we accomplish this? My gut told me that we would be able to succeed, but there had to be a better path. What were we missing? I could feel my head pounding as I rounded the corner toward my office.

"Sarah, could you grab me another cup of coffee, please? It's going to be a long day!"

Congratulations you started your journey to become an analytic leader. The fact you are reading this book indicates you are already more advanced than many of your peers. I am committed to guiding you to lead your organization through the data revolution and transforming it with data and analytics.

Throughout this book, the characters will utilize tools I have created and have made available to you for free. Simply register at www.Heatherized.com/bookbonus, and you will gain access to many tools to aid you in your journey to become an analytic leader! Periodically, the material will be updated to help you advance your skills.

Here is what you'll receive:

- BI Action Assessment Indicator
- Core Values worksheet
- Questionnaires
- Sample job description for attracting BI superstars
- Videos to improve communication and provide time-saving methods
- And more!

Sign up today at www.Heatherized.com/BookBonus.

CHAPTER 2

Are You an Analytic Leader?

"When the student is ready, the teacher will appear."

–Unknown

It had been a week since my discussion with Chris and Bob, and the conversation kept popping into my mind. It appeared again as I rode in an Uber to the Tampa airport to catch a flight to San Diego. I'd given a lot of thought to how we were going to transform our company. As a distribution company, our employees really didn't like change. Many feared technologies. There had to be a better way to create a cultural shift.

The last year had been challenging. Our sales were flat, and we were losing market share in some areas. All the articles I read stated that the companies that learn to transform their businesses to leverage data will dominate their markets. What if our competition figures out how to successfully leverage data better than us and start using artificial intelligence that could put us out of business? This is a massive challenge. I began to wonder, "Is this data and technology stuff even worth me focusing on? I'm only five years from retirement. Maybe I should just leave the transformation for my successor. Maybe we could just continue business as usual. Wouldn't that be easier?"

I hopped out of the Uber. I thanked the driver and headed to my gate. I had just enough time to grab a Starbucks before boarding.

At least that would give me the energy to get some work done on the plane. I often found I got more done on planes than sitting in an office because it was uninterrupted time.

As I approached the gate and observed all the people, I thought to myself, "This must be a full flight. At least my upgrade came through." Shortly thereafter, I boarded the plane and got settled in my aisle seat. Most of the plane had boarded, and I thought, "Wow, maybe the seat next to me is empty," when a cheerful woman with bright green eyes and light brown hair said, "Excuse me. I'm in the window seat."

"Oh, sure. Hold on a sec," I said as I stood up to get out of her way.

"Phew, I thought I might miss the flight," she said. "You ever have one of those days when you're just a little behind?"

"Seems like that that's the norm these days," I said.

There was something different about her. She wore dark jeans and a dark purple sweater that made her eyes sparkle. She had an energy about her. You know how every now and then, you meet someone, and their energy is contagious? She sat down and settled herself, grabbing a large white book out of her bag before pushing the brown leather bag under the seat in front of her with her foot. I glanced over to see what she was reading and noticed it said "Predictive Analytics" on the spine.

"So, are you going to San Diego on business or for pleasure?" she asked.

"Oh, I'm just going in for a couple days for business meetings. How about yourself?"

"I'm headed there for a conference. But it should be a lot of fun, and I love the Gaslamp District," she said as she adjusted her seatbelt.

"What kind of a conference?" I asked. Normally, I wouldn't be so talkative, but for some reason, I felt the need to talk to her. Maybe it was the book that intrigued me.

She laughed as she said, "I'm going to Brendon Burchard's High-Performance Academy. Have you heard of him? He's the author of the book *High Performance Habits: How Extraordinary People Become That Way.*" I shook my head no, and she explained that Brendon is kind of like Tony Robbins but focuses more on business and sharing your expertise. Apparently, he's done a lot of research on what makes certain people and organizations high performers.

"Wow, that sounds very interesting. I think we all could use something to make us more productive."

"Yes, the methods he teaches are amazing. However, what I love the most is meeting all the interesting people there. There are executives, consultants, doctors, artists, life coaches, healers, and musicians. It's a really diverse crowd, but all are lifelong learners. In a strange way, it's the one place I feel like I belong," she laughed. "So, what do you do?" she asked.

"I'm in the distribution business," I said. "Not exactly an exciting industry."

"So, I take it you like a challenge?" she said. "From what I know, the distribution industry is getting highly competitive. You have retailers who want to pay less while they want you to do a lot more for them so they can meet the demands of their demanding customers. Right?"

"Exactly," I said.

"And are you also experiencing that the manufacturers are trying to ship direct to the customer?" she asked.

"Yes, that's a challenge. It seems like you know a lot about distribution."

"I have a few customers that are in the distribution industry. I'm curious. What do you find are your biggest challenges?"

"Hmm, there so many challenges. But I think right now, our biggest challenge is achieving sustainable growth. We have spurts, but then we lose market share."

"Why do you think that's happening?"

"I am not sure. If I knew, I would work to fix it. Sometimes, it seems as if our competitors have inside knowledge on accounts that helps them beat us."

She nodded her head. "Are you familiar with the data revolution?"

"Hmm, kind of. Isn't that where companies use big data and robots?"

"Some argue that the data revolution could have as big effect on the world as the industrial revolution," she said as her eyes got as big as saucers. "There are many different definitions, but basically, it is the transformative world we are in where data is an asset that should be leveraged to make timely decisions, monitor progress, and automate everything, even self-driving cars. On a basic level, data used wisely can not only increase profits but can help companies conquer market share by providing better goods and services. On a more advanced level, it can automate and analyze data with machine learning so much faster than humans. The possibilities are endless. Data is becoming a huge asset to organizations that collect and protect it. Any chance your competitors are using data to win deals?"

"You know, we are attempting to leverage data, but it's just our business intelligence initiative. Not sure if that counts in the data revolution," I said.

"Attempting? Sounds like it's not as successful as you would like."

"No, definitely not. It's been a struggle. From what you described, the data revolution isn't just using business intelligence tools wisely."

"Well, BI is one part of it. Business intelligence tools, as most people refer to them, leverage data as a view of what happened and report on actuals that happened in the prior month. With the data revolution, it's not about just looking at what happened. It is using data to optimize performance, leveraging machines to analyze data, and providing a prediction of what will happen. If we let machines do the heavy lifting for us, we can make more informed decisions. The machines even go a step further and execute tasks based on the data. Machines can assess what happened, predict what will happen, and then act or do a tasked based on the data. Like a child, the machines keep learning and improving."

"You mean like artificial intelligence?" I asked.

"Yes. You have heard all the hype about robots, self-driving cars, and artificial intelligence, right?"

"Yes, of course. *60 Minutes* even had a special on it."[1]

"Yeah, they did. At the most basic level, all it involves is machines taking in data, analyzing it, and deciding what to do or making recommendations based on what they learned in the past. So, a self-driving car is really taking in millions of data points and responding to what it sees and knows base on learning to drive the car. Have you heard of IBM's Watson?"

"Of course, they advertise it on the Golf Channel," I laughed.

"In healthcare, Watson is learning the information in thousands of medical journals a day, and then, when it's provided with patient data, it's making recommendations. I saw a guy from the University of Tokyo present on how they had a patient that was dying of leukemia, and they were treating her, but she wasn't responding to the treatment. The team of doctors let Watson look at the records, and in 10 minutes, Watson compared the patient's genetic changes with a database of 20 million cancer research papers. It's estimated that it would have taken two weeks for human scientists to identify which of the 1,000 changes were diagnostically important or not. Watson flew through the data. It turns out she did have leukemia but a different form, and it needed a different treatment. The new treatment put her in remission.[2] Pretty powerful stuff!"

"Wow, that's amazing. Hmm, that explains why the board is asking us what our plans are with artificial intelligence."

"Many executives I work with are concerned that if they don't figure out how to use artificial intelligence and analytics that their competitors will figure it out, and the effects could be devastating for the laggards. Personally, I believe companies that seek sustainable increased profits must look at their AI and analytics roadmap as a key component to achieving their goals."

"Mmmm," I moaned. "Yeah, the data revolution scares me. I keep reading articles about how we need to become a data and analytics-driven company. We need to start leveraging predictive and artificial intelligence. Heck, even our board is talking about artificial intelligence. But candidly, I don't know where to start. There are so many different terms, and I don't even really know what they all mean. My last statistics class was 30 years ago," I stated as I laughed. "I couldn't help but notice your book. What do you do?"

The tall, thin flight attendant interrupted our conversation by offering a beverage before taking off. "Yes, I'll take a coffee with cream and sugar because my friend here didn't bring me a Starbucks," said the woman as she flashed a flirtatious smile. "Well, ironically, I am a Business Analytics Advisor to executives. So, basically, I help them create a roadmap to transform their companies to be data and analytics-driven. It's a blast. I have the best job in the world."

"Well, that explains why you're reading a book on predictive analytics," I said, pointing to the book.

"Yeah, pretty nerdy, don't you think? I like to keep up with what the various experts are saying about our industry. Actually, this is a great book. You might want to check it out," she said as she waved the book.[3]

"Besides figuring out data and analytics, you said your challenge is sustainable profits and market share, right?"

"Definitely. We are losing market share. We are being outbid by our competitors, and as you stated, the manufacturers are trying to sell direct."

"How are you solving that problem?"

"We're trying to get better visibility into the cost of deliveries. Trying to calculate customer and location profitability is a primary focus. But we are finding it challenging to get what we need out of our current business intelligence tools. When we do receive the data, it only shows us there's a problem. We can't drill down to see why things are off. I believe we have a great IT team. They just seem to be struggling. When they roll out new reports and dashboards, for some reason, the end users don't use it."

"How long have you been trying to solve this problem?"

"A couple years, believe it or not."

"Why do you think IT is failing?"

"I don't really know. But my CIO keeps saying he is handcuffed by not having a data warehouse. I don't get what good that would do. We have so much data. We are drowning in data but have no insight," I said, showing my frustration.

"You know, a lot of companies struggle. You're not alone. Heck, that's what keeps me in business," she smiled. "I find a lot of executives believe that funding a BI project is enough. They think that IT should be able to roll out tools that help them make better decisions. But, business intelligence doesn't work that way. There are number of factors that all have to be in alignment to realize success. It's amazing how many of my CFO friends gripe about the expense of BI, and when I ask them if they use dashboards, they say they prefer to double-check the numbers, so they do things in Excel. What kind of role model is that?" she said, shaking her head. "I strongly believe that companies that deploy business intelligence and artificial intelligence will conquer market share and increase productivity. But many companies are reluctant to do what it takes to truly transform their organizations."

Now, I was intrigued. What did she mean by "do what it takes?"

"So, what do you think it takes to succeed?" I asked.

"I believe that business intelligence success is determined by how companies handle four main components of BI: people, processes, data, and tools. For most companies, people are the most challenging component and why BI fails. You see, when we rely on IT to define and deliver business intelligence, it's kind of like mowing the lawn with hedge trimmers. Many IT professionals are introverted. We studied computer science in school to hide behind a computer. But technology today has pushed IT professionals into the forefront of corporate change. We are asking IT professionals to connect with the business to collaborate, yet many are lacking the social skills necessary. Have you ever noticed how the business thinks IT people are rude?"

"Ha, yes. They do come off a little curt."

"And IT people often think the business people are too stupid to understand the technology. The real problem is that they communicate in a completely different language. To top it off, many IT people are highly analytical. Analytically minded people have brains that are wired to solve problems. When an IT person sits down to define requirements for a new dashboard, they ask the user what they want on the dashboard, and they immediately start to design and solve the problem in their head. Unfortunately, many times, the most important information is shared by the user much later in the conversation. But the IT professional never really hears the important stuff because their brain is occupied building solutions."

"Wow, that makes a lot of sense. Finance people are like that too," I laughed. "I do find it challenging to communicate with some of our IT team members. It's as if they aren't listening, and they give me these looks like I am an idiot."

"And, to make matters worse, most executives don't give IT the proper time to communicate the strategic goals of the company. When I teach classes to business intelligence professionals, I always ask how many attendees can clearly articulate the strategic goals of their organization. Guess what percentage raise their hands?"

"I don't know. Maybe 10%?" I said.

"I wish it was that high. Less than 4% of BI professionals can clearly articulate the strategic direction of their company. And yet, executives and business units expect IT to deliver dashboards and reports to help the organization drive toward and achieve the strategic goals. It's like they expect IT to run a marathon, but they never tell them where the finish line is. Then they wonder why IT can't finish the race."

I looked down. "Wow. That is exactly what we're doing," I said. I sat there for a moment in silence, contemplating the fact that our BI failure was my failure. The roar of the engines filled my head. I had been so deep in conversation that I hadn't even realized we were already up in the air.

"You're not alone! Most companies don't realize they set their IT departments up for failure. The good news is that the issue is primarily a communication problem—a problem created by both IT and the business. It's a problem I believe can be resolved by teaching communication and social skills to IT. I joke that my real job is socializing the nerds," she said, flipping her hair. "Oh, and I can say that because I am one of them. I studied finance and computer science in school. You don't get much geekier."

"I like that," I laughed. "Socializing the nerds. Well, our IT team could use a little socializing. Curious, how did you get into this?"

"I guess you could say I was born into it. My parents had a software firm when I was a kid. My dad created one of the first software packages to track the futures market on a real-time basis in the early 80s. It was a family business, so I started working in software as a teenager, training futures traders how to use a computer. The software provided charts of the markets and trend analysis. I have been in analytics and business intelligence most of my life."

"That's pretty impressive. But I don't see you as a nerd that needs socializing." I smile.

"Well, I used to be. Thousands of self-help books and personal development courses later, and I am a socialized nerd. Yes, I am a personal development junkie. That's why I am going to San Diego."

"I need to do more of that," I said. "Can I ask you a stupid question?"

"Sure, but there are no stupid questions."

"When you talk about business intelligence, what exactly do you mean? How do you define it? I find some people just think it's reporting, while some say it includes performance management and planning. In our company, we really are just trying to get basic reporting automated and calling it business intelligence."

"When I say 'business intelligence,' I don't just mean reports and pretty visualizations. I personally believe that business intelligence must encompass a continuous loop solution that includes reporting and dashboarding so you can see how you've done. That's like using a rearview mirror to see where you have been. It should also include data mining and analysis to drill into details and see why something happened. But then, you need to see where you are going. So, you need predictive and prescriptive analytics where you leverage machine learning and artificial intelligence to give you a view of the future. And from that information, you need to be able to adjust your forecasts and plans. The forecasts, which some call performance management, should be interconnected. When you change the forecast for marketing, you better see an effect on the sales numbers, but many companies still have siloed forecasts and plans for the various departments."

"So, you think the business intelligence is all of it? I have read that some people think artificial intelligence is separate."

"Think about it. Artificial intelligence is reliant on clean data, and the point of AI is to give you insights into your business based on the existing data. But with AI, a machine learns from the data and then predicts the future. In the past, we hired people to look at the data and predict the future. The difference is a machine can learn at a fast pace and scan much more data than a human can. And the machine is not influenced by human emotion; it just looks at the facts. There are some interesting studies about parole board rulings, and if the parole board is hungry, the person will probably stay in prison. Machines don't get hungry." She smiled. "So, yes, I think AI is a component of business intelligence. I am afraid that companies that struggle with BI will have an even greater challenge with AI."

"Ouch, that hurt," I said as I laughed. "You are basically telling me that I am going to fail at AI since we have failed at BI."

"No, you can succeed. I think any organization can succeed, but they must learn how to succeed, and more importantly, the executives need to be willing to take the difficult steps necessary to succeed."

"You've kind of implied twice now that the executives aren't doing what is necessary. How so?"

"Executives need to learn the secrets to BI success and then fully support their teams. Most executives don't know how to be analytic leaders and, unfortunately, most consulting firms that advise companies don't want them to know the secrets because it would hurt their businesses. Fewer billable hours," she said, raising her eyebrows.

"I assume you know the secret to success, then?" I asked.

"My clients think so," she said with a slight smile. "I've been doing this a long time, and I am tired of seeing good people and organizations fail. A couple of years ago, I was so frustrated that I thought about a career change. I would tell clients how to be successful with business intelligence, but they would pick and choose which recommendations they wanted to implement and wonder why they were not successful. This is like going on a diet but refusing to stop drinking alcohol every day and wondering why the diet doesn't work. I'd tell the clients that executive engagement is crucial, and they would say, 'Well, that's not going to happen, they are too busy.' I didn't know how to get through to them. It threw me in a rut, and I was feeling very unfulfilled. Have you ever felt that way in your career?"

"I know exactly how you felt. I've been in a rut! I felt like I was on a treadmill going nowhere, making no progress, and feeling sort of empty. I found myself wondering if there is something more in life."

"That's exactly the feeling. I felt stuck and was getting depressed. Then, one day, a girlfriend called and asked me to go to a Tony Robbins event with her. Do you know who he is? He's the really tall motivational guy."

"Yeah." I smiled, nodded my head, and thought about his role in the movie *Shallow Hal*.

"Well, when she asked me to go with her, I laughed and said, 'I hear he makes you hug strangers, and I'm not a hugger.' She pleaded with me and then recommended I watch Oprah Winfrey's special on Tony Robbins. After watching it, I figured if Oprah could do it, so could I. A month later, I sat in a huge conference hall in San Jose, California, filled with over five thousand people at the *Unleash the Power Within* event. Everyone there was looking to make changes in their life. They were looking for something more. As I sat there, I witnessed Tony explain why people fail to make the changes they want the most. Then, he provided a repeatable, proven framework to take massive action to make the desired changes.

"All of a sudden, it was like lightning struck, and I decided I wanted to be the Tony Robbins of data and analytics. How geeky is that? I realized that the organizations that are trying to make changes to become data and analytics-driven are struggling because they don't have a framework. I decided at that moment that I would create a framework for BI professionals to succeed that every client could implement. Most organizations focus on the business intelligence tools and whether they meet their needs. However, people and open communication are the secrets to success. My framework addresses the communication problem. Most of my friends think I am nuts, but I am cool with that," she said, bobbing her head.

"After Tony, I immediately started working with clients in IT and giving them my framework, and the people that committed to it saw amazing results. But then, I realized I was missing a piece. I was working with IT and BI professionals, but they were handcuffed by executives who were not communicating or engaged in the initiative. Most executives do not know how to become analytic leaders. So, I added analytic leadership to my framework." Her eyes sparkled and flashed complete confidence that was almost contagious. Clearly, this was her passion.

"So, do you think your executives know how to become analytic leaders?" she asked me.

"Clearly not!" I blurted as the sinking feeling that I was a big part of the problem overcame me.

"Well, that's the first step. You need to get your executives to realize they have a problem, and then get them to commit to solving it. That's usually the biggest challenge. Do you have an executive in your company that could be a BI champion? Ideally, it would be the CEO, but it can be the Chief Financial Officer or the Chief Operating Officer. I don't recommend the CIO or CTO be your champion. You need an executive from the business."

"Well, if the champion needs to have knowledge and an understanding of analytics, I would say our CFO is probably the best. He has a computer science and finance background like you."

"That's fabulous. That's not the most common background, but it's definitely an asset! The executive doesn't need to have knowledge or experience. They just need to have the desire to make a big change and be willing to be engage in and commit to the process. Everything else can be learned. Oh, and a little political capital or influence doesn't hurt either," she said.

"I'm a little confused. What's the role of the champion, and why couldn't the CIO be the champion?"

"Sounds like you have been expecting the CIO to be the champion. And how's that working for you?" she winked.

"The reason the CIO shouldn't be your champion is that IT needs the engagement of the business. Business users are notorious for not communicating their real needs and not understanding what's possible. They expect IT to wave the magic wand and figure it out. If the champion is an executive from the business and they take the time to become an analytic leader, they can help bridge the chasm between IT and the business. Ideally, your team is not just IT. It's a mix of business, IT, data integration specialists, and maybe a data scientist. The champion must be committed to change, do things that may not be popular at the time, and have a vision of business intelligence success. The champion should view data and analytics as critical to the company's long-term success, and they should want to have analytic leadership as their legacy."

"I think I need to be it!" I blurted out a little louder than I expected.

"I am sorry. I am not following."

"I am the executive that needs to be committed to making a change. Just this morning, I was asking myself if it's worth pursuing the changes needed to become, as you say, data and analytics-driven. You know, I am only five years from retirement. But you have given me hope! I am optimistic that you are as good as you come across," I said. As I looked her in the eyes, I noticed that she blushed and looked a little embarrassed.

"Oh, I am sorry. I didn't know you were an executive. Most executives put their Bose noise-cancelling headphones on and don't want to talk on a plane," she smiled.

"Funny. I usually am that guy," I smiled. "I am the CEO. But I guess I am not an analytic leader—at least not yet." Something in my gut told me I needed to commit to learning more about data and analytics. Something had to change, so why not start with me?

"Not yet!" She flashed her green eyes and a brilliant smile. "That's fabulous! You know, I talk with a lot of executives that are facing the dilemma you are. It takes a big cultural shift to become a data and analytics-driven organization."

"Yes, I am starting to see that."

"The secret to shifting the organization is to shift the mindset of the executives first. Once they engage and embrace data and analytics, the organization will follow. I get asked a lot if it's worth the time, money, and effort to create the cultural shift needed. Like you, some ask if they should just leave it to their successor. I have to say, based on our limited interaction, you seem like the type of guy who genuinely wants to leave a legacy. If you were to close your eyes and envision yourself when you retire, what do you see? How do you want to leave your company?"

I sat in silence, thinking about my retirement. I hadn't thought about it but, of course, I want to leave on top. But if we keep struggling the way we have been, I might be asked to leave.

"You don't seem like the type who wants to retire leaving a flat company, or worse, a struggling company that could be forced to lay off. Imagine how it would feel to leave your company on your terms when it's dominating the market. Imagine the board begging you to say for a few more years."

"That would be amazing!" I visualized walking into the company and having everyone excited, getting the numbers, and knowing we were dominating our market. I opened my eyes. "Wow, you've inspired me! I do want to go out on top! How do I get started?"

She laughed. "Before you commit to this, I want to ask you a very important question. You might want to close your eyes for this too." I closed my eyes. "I want you to really think about this before you answer. Who is counting on you to lead them? The other executives, all your employees, maybe your vendors and customers? Picture the people. Picture their families that count on their income to survive. Now, imagine if your leadership helped them go from surviving to thriving. How would you feel?"

I was overcome with pride. I pictured the office buzzing with happy people. I opened my eyes, and I suddenly realized I was sitting next to this person that could help my company, and I didn't even know who she was. "Oh my God, I am sorry. I don't even know you name," I snickered. "I am James Brown, the CEO of Playfair Distributing." I reached out my hand to shake her hand. "And you are?"

"Well, hello James Brown, it's a pleasure to meet you. I am Ally Canfield, a Business Analytics Advisor and high-performance coach." We laughed as we shook hands.

"No, the pleasure is all mine."

Key Takeaways:

- The data revolution is happening now. It is the transformative world we are in where data is an asset that should be leveraged to make timely decisions, monitor progress, and automate everything, including self-driving cars.

- Successful business intelligence requires four key components: people, processes, tools, and data.

- Communication and people are the secret sauce to business intelligence.

- Business intelligence should be a continuous loop that includes reporting, dashboarding, data mining, analysis, predictive and prescriptive analytics, and forecasting.

- Business intelligence success requires executives that are willing to be engage in and commit to the process of change, not just sponsor BI initiatives and rely on IT.

- Executives need to become analytic leaders.

You are proving you want to be an analytic leader and transform your organization. The data revolution is a huge opportunity for those that do the work and commit to change and you are proving to be one of them. Remember, I am committed to guiding you. If you have not signed up for the bonus material I created for this book, I strongly recommend you do it now.

Simply register at www.Heatherized.com/bookbonus, and you will gain access to many tools to aid you in your journey to become an analytic leader!

Here is what you'll receive:

- BI Action Assessment Indicator
- Core Values worksheet
- Questionnaires
- Sample job description for attracting BI superstars
- Videos to improve communication and provide time-saving methods
- And more!

Sign up today at www.Heatherized.com/BookBonus.

CHAPTER 3

Learning the Basics

"Being ignorant is not so much a shame,
as being unwilling to learn."

–Benjamin Franklin

"Seriously Ally, what do I need to do? How do we get started?"

"Well, if you were to engage me as your Business Analytics Advisor, we would first need to get you confident in the jargon of analytics and get an understanding of the moving parts. Too many executives think they can just rely on the CIO, and they can't. To be an analytic leader, you need to know the basics and what questions to ask. Then, I would advise you on how to get your executive team excited about business intelligence and analytics and assess where your organization is today. Once the executives agree and commit to doing what it takes to lead the cultural transformation, we would go through my framework that I call the '*Business Intelligence Bull's-eye Framework.*'"

"This is exciting. I like the name." Ally gave me an awkward smile as if there was something she was holding back. "So, how do I learn what I need to know? The jargon and basics? Candidly, this stuff makes me uneasy. I really don't want to look ignorant. Before this flight, I thought I was doing the right thing by delegating it to IT."

"Well, typically, we do a foundations exercise with the entire team to make sure everyone is on the same page and that we all use the same definitions. Since this is a long flight and I don't really feel like reading, I could explain the basics for you now if you like."

"Really? That would be fabulous!"

Ally reached into her large brown leather bag under the seat and pulled out a manila folder from which she grabbed a few blank sheets of paper. She then pulled out a small plastic pouch containing thin colored markers. "I like color," she said with a sheepish grin. "They say color and pictures helps wake up the right side of our brains—you know, the creative side. Do you mind if I assume you know nothing? I find that's usually the easiest way to make sure we don't miss anything."

"I really don't know much, so that's a great place to start."

She started by drawing two cylinders, above which she drew two puffy clouds. "It all starts with the data," she said as she wrote the word "data" in the cylinders. "These represent just a few of your many data sources. You have data in your ERP (enterprise resource planning) system, your CRM (customer relationship management) system, and many others. That data could be what we call on-premise, meaning you have it on servers in your organization, or they could be in the cloud and hosted somewhere like Salesforce."

"Yes, we have both," I said. "We have tons of data."

"Yes, most companies do, but the challenge is that there is so much data that it's hard to organize and, therefore, it's not useable. Have you ever seen the television show about people who hoard?" she asked.

"Yes, that's a disturbing show. It's kind of like watching a train wreck. You don't want to watch, but you can't not," I laughed. "Why?"

"Well, most companies are data hoarders. They have so much of stuff, they can't find what they need when they need it. Because it's so disorganized, it causes friction among people just like hoarding causes friction and disagreements between family members of hoarders. But to make matters worse, with data, there are different definitions depending on who you talk to. Have you ever had a conversation with someone from the UK? It's amazing how many English words have a completely different definition in the UK than in the US."

"Like a shopping cart is called a trolley, or football is soccer," I stated.

"Exactly. Well, data has a similar problem. For example, some divisions may define sales as sales before returns and allowances, and other divisions may say it's after returns and allowances. When you have a meeting in which people report their sales, the calculations could be completely different."

"Oh, that's us! We sit in meetings arguing why the numbers are different. That's why we spend hundreds of thousands of dollars on a top-rated business intelligence tool. We were told it would give us one version of the truth. It's supposed to generate reports and dashboards that include all of our data," I explained.

Ally laughed and said, "Sounds like you've drunk the software sales professional Kool-Aid. BI solutions can deliver one version of the truth, and they can report off many data sources. When my clients ask me if they can report off-source data from multiple sources, I tell them they are asking the wrong question. The question to ask is not, 'can I?' The question you should ask is, 'should I?'"

With a shocked look on my face I asked, "What?" The thought that we may be going about it incorrectly filled my head.

"You see, when you report off many data sources with your BI tool, you have to make sure the data definitions in the different systems are the same. The definition of sales in one system may be different than in another. Or a customer in one system may have included all their locations, whereas another system may have the locations as separate customer numbers. Therefore, the definitions in disparate systems need to be standardized. Unfortunately, without a data warehouse and strong data governance, the person writing the report must use a lot of what I call 'duct tape and super glue' by coding the report to standardize the data. This creates a lot more work and is extremely error-prone. Your typical end users couldn't create a report that's accurate. If you have bad data or data that is not clean, which often happens when reporting off many systems in one report, then it pretty much kills any hopes of deploying self-service BI where the end users can create their own reports and dashboard."

I felt as if someone just punched me in the stomach. I sat in silence for a moment, processing it all. Here we were hundreds of thousands of dollars into our BI investment, and we were duct taping and super gluing. "I am pretty sure we are using a lot of duct tape. Why didn't anyone tell us?" I asked.

"I am sorry. I don't mean to upset you. You are not alone. You see, software salespeople are paid to sell software. They did not lie to you. Their software most likely can report off many disparate systems. What you need to realize is that most salespeople have never implemented BI. They are not consultants. They might not know the best practice is to have an enterprise data warehouse and define data policies that correctly stage the data from the subsystems. I think most salespeople think the consultants implementing your solution should make the recommendations for your unique situation. Don't feel bad. A lot of people go down the multi-source path. It has its purpose, but it's not optimal for a long-term solution or if you want to deploy self-service BI. I am guessing your IT department recommended a data warehouse, but because of the language barrier, maybe you didn't understand what they were saying or why a data warehouse was important."

"Hmm, Bob, our CIO, has been disgruntled with Chris, our CFO, because he never gets funding for a data warehouse," I said with a contemplative look on my face. "That's why he's asking for funding."

"Yes, I bet it is. I have a client that distributes auto parts. When I started working with them a number of years ago, I took the CFO, Matt, to a BI conference, and he saw the dashboards. I thought he was going to jump out of his chair when he saw what was possible.

He said he had to have dashboards. The next day, I call the CIO, a brilliant man named Gerry. I told Gerry that I took Matt to a conference where he saw BI dashboards. I said, 'He is willing to buy you some new BI tools to play with if he can get a financial dashboard. Do you support this?' I was expecting a 'heck yes' from him, but he said, 'No, absolutely not.' I was shocked! 'What? Why?' I asked Gerry. Gerry said, 'No, I can't support this and will be adamant against it.'

"Gerry explained that he had been asking for funding for a data warehouse for five years, like Bob," Ally said with snarky smile. "But Matt always rejected him. There is no way he could deliver BI on bad data. That could kill the company if people made decisions based on it. Gerry was absolutely right."

"So then, I asked, 'Gerry, if I can get your data warehouse project funded, would you support this initiative?' He responded that he would definitely support it and would love new state-of-the-art BI tools if he had good data. You see, Gerry just wasn't speaking the same language as his CFO, but they wanted the same thing. When Gerry was asking Matt for a data warehouse, he never explained what the benefit to the CFO would be in terms the CFO understood. I told Gerry I had a plan to get him a data warehouse. He was skeptical at first, but I told Gerry to update his numbers. I needed him to know exactly what the data warehouse project would cost, what resources he needed, and his timeline for his data warehouse project."

"I then called a meeting with Gerry and Matt. At the meeting, I demoed the dashboards, and Matt got excited. Then, I turned and asked Gerry if he supported the project. As we planned, he said 'no' and explained what would happen if he put BI on their bad data. Then, I asked Gerry what he needed to fix the data. Gerry pitched the request for a data warehouse, sharing the cost, timeline, and resources he needed. Matt responded that he had no idea that dashboards and reporting were why Gerry wanted the data warehouse and approved the project using 'special funds' within 45 minutes of the start of the meeting. So, you see, you are not alone."

I felt relieved. "Basically, you are telling me we need to fund a data warehousing project. Doesn't that take years?"

"It could take a long time. I may have oversimplified things a bit," Ally said. "You see, organizations need to look at data differently. They need to view it as precious—something to be cared for and protected. The challenge is that a lot of people think data is IT's responsibility and that IT owns it. But the truth is that the business owns the data. IT protects the data. They are like the knights protecting the castle. The business needs to commit to working with IT to clean up the data and communicate how they want to use the data. A data warehouse helps, but companies really need to develop a complete plan and roadmap just for data, including data governance and data integration. Typically, there are so many systems in different locations. Some are in the cloud, and then, if an organization acquires another company, it can get very messy. Data is an organization's treasure to be guarded by the knights. That's why a lot of companies are bringing Chief Data Officers on board."

I could feel my eyes rolling into the back of my head! I felt as if I was drinking from a fire hose. How would we ever be successful? This was going to cost a fortune, and for what return?

"You look concerned," said Ally, patting my arm. "Don't worry. It's not that bad. I realize that this can be overwhelming if you are new to it. It sounded like you have standardized on one BI tool, is that correct?"

"Kind of. We have IBM Cognos, but the CFO wants to buy Tableau."

"It's not uncommon for companies to have multiple solutions, especially with acquisitions. That's why it's so important to create a business intelligence roadmap that is flexible. You don't want to spend money on tools you don't need, but you need to meet the demands of the business."

"What do your clients with multiple systems do?"

"Some keep multiple systems, while some standardize so IT doesn't have to support so many systems and they don't pay as much in licensing support fees. Others buy tools that sit on top of multiple business intelligence systems and standardizes the end user interface so they don't have to change their BI tools. There are tools like Motio's Theia that do this. This is great option for companies that are in acquisition mode."

"How do they decide what's best?"

"If they are smart, they bring in a Business Analytics Advisor like me," Ally winked.

"I still wonder if all the cost is worth it," I said, shaking my head.

"You know, a lot of executives wonder if all the cost and effort is worth it. It's not uncommon for companies to call me after their executives tell the BI team that they have one year to be successful and show value or they will scrap BI all together. That's why I created the MacGyver approach," Ally said.

"The MacGyver approach? What's that?" I asked.

"Do you remember the 1980s TV show *MacGyver*?"

"Yes, actually, I think it's back on the air."

"Well, MacGyver was a spy, and he would get into precarious situations that he needed to get out of immediately. He was the master of using what was available at the time to solve the problem. Usually, it was a shoestring, duct tape, a match, and bubble gum," she laughed.

"Yes, I love MacGyver."

"Admit it. You wanted to be him," Ally teased. "I believe executives need immediate results. They won't spend years trying to get business intelligence up while spending tons of money."

"I like what you are saying."

"I believe that companies need to use a MacGyver approach to data and analytics. With the MacGyver approach, you define the most important situation to solve and do it rapidly. It should be something that completely moves the needle and increases profits. To start, the team focuses on one thing. They need a quick win."

"That makes sense. The team proves the value of BI."

"Exactly. I hosted a workshop recently where a client that used my MacGyver process defined a dashboard that when deployed to the end users was estimated to make the company over $1.2 million a year. And that was recurring revenue, not a one-hit wonder."

"From one dashboard? $1.2 million?"

"Yes. Apparently, there was information the salespeople needed but was taking two months to deliver. They figured out how to leverage a data mart and deliver the information weekly, allowing the salespeople to identify low-hanging fruit. They estimated that with buying software and paying consultants, the initial cost to build the dashboard was going to cost about $200,000. They figured it would take about 90 days to deliver."

"I'll take that kind of return," I laughed.

"The trick to the MacGyver approach is that we deliver what we call a 'minimal viable product (MVP).' This allows you to test an idea, prove it adds the expected value before you fully invest time and money in the solution. With MacGyver, we accept that this is not the best long-term method, and we know we will implement 'best practices' when the solution is proven to add value. The minimal viable product is like a pilot of the idea that doesn't have all the bells and whistles that we will ultimately want."

"If we return to the drawing, we will add data marts. A data mart is subset of a data warehouse that is usually oriented to a specific line of business. It's like a baby data warehouse. We may end up creating a few data marts as we go along. Eventually we will use the data marts to form the enterprise data warehouse," she said as she drew two more squares with arrows coming from the data clouds and data cylinders. Through the tail of the arrow, she wrote "ETL." She then drew a large data cylinder with arrows from the data marts to the large cylinder now labeled "data warehouse."

"To deliver under the MacGyver approach, it's not uncommon to need a data mart that holds the data you will need for the specific initiative. Just remember, at a later date, the long-term goal would be to pull this data into the enterprise data warehouse."

"I think we have some data marts now," I said.

"Yes, you probably do. Reporting directly off source systems is not recommended because it can cause performance issues in your source system. If I put a BI tool on top of your GL system, it could cause the GL system to slow down. When the BI report is run, it's going to call on resources from the GL system. The more reports and queries performed directly off the source system, the slower the source system will be. It's like a traffic jam. Needless to say, that's not good at month-end."

"Think about it," she continued. "When software companies create software like an ERP system, the data is stored in a way that is optimized for the task the software is doing, not necessarily for reporting. As I mentioned earlier, when you have multiple systems, the systems may not have the same definitions, like with the definition of sales. It's also common for different systems to have different codes for the same item. For example, a client number may be six characters in one system and eight characters in another. This can cause challenges for reporting, so we use a little process to match things up. This process is called 'ETL,' which stands for 'extract, transform, and load.' Basically, it pulls the data from the source systems, transforms it so we use one definition, and then, it loads it to a data mart, which could be SQL or some other database. By starting with the data marts instead of starting with a huge enterprise data warehouse project, you get to test drive how you want to use the data before you spend a ton of money and time on designing the enterprise data warehouse."

"I like the idea of test driving," I said.

"Yes, it's important to understand how the users will use the data because a good data warehouse needs to be indexed properly."

"Indexed?"

"Yes, I believe lack of indexing is the one of the main reason users are frustrated with reporting tools. Have you ever clicked on a report and it appears to sit and spin for a long time before it renders?"

"Yes, all the time. I joke with Sarah, my assistant, that the system needs more coffee."

"Well, that's because the report is having to do a lot of work to find the information you asked for. The combination of duct tape and super glue coding in the report with a poorly indexed data mart or data warehouse causes the system to have to work really hard. Indexing your data mart or warehouse is like having a clean garage. Have you ever let your garage go and there's just stuff everywhere?" Ally asked.

"Yes, have you been in my garage recently?" I laughed.

"Let's say your garage is a mess, and your wife wants you to put air in the grandkids' bikes before they arrive. You go to the garage to look for the bike pump and feel completely overwhelmed."

I smiled and said, "I can completely relate. Half the time, when I am looking for something, I find it's just easiest to run down the street to Lowe's to buy a new one."

"Which just adds to the clutter," she said with a wink. "You could spend hours looking for the bike pump, or as you do, you could buy a new one. But what if, instead, your garage was completely organized and everything had its place? The items you use regularly were very accessible, and you just had to walk to the garage and grab the pump."

"That would be fabulous."

"Well, that is indexing. It's a way to tell the system where the data you are requesting is hiding. Indexing makes the questions you ask of the data render quickly."

With a slight frown on my face, I said, "I am pretty sure we aren't indexed. So, I have a question. Is my IT department lacking skills? Shouldn't they know this stuff?"

"Great questions. They probably do. They have probably brought this up to the business units, but IT can't work in a vacuum. Defining data structures and even knowing how to index things takes collaboration. Imagine if I went in and cleaned your garage without understanding what you use often and what you want in long-term storage. I would probably put your stand-up paddleboards at the front so they are easily accessible because I love to paddleboard. Whereas, your golf clubs would go in the back in long-term storage. But you might be a golfer, and you would want your golf clubs accessible. If we don't communicate before I clean your garage, it won't be optimized for your needs. Similarly, it takes communication before IT can index your data. They aren't really good at reading your mind," she said.

"So, why doesn't IT just ask us how we want to use it?"

"My guess is they have, but again, the language barrier is so great. There's often a communication breakdown. IT isn't always great at discovering requirements, but it's not their fault. Most have not been trained in requirements discovery. When I studied computer science, we were never taught how to facilitate discussions or how to get business users to share their ideas. Since most business users are not tech-savvy, we tend to assume they won't know what they need anyway. That's why training your IT people on facilitation is so key. Requirements need to be discovered. They can't be gathered because the end users don't always know what they need from new technology."

"Yeah, our IT folks aren't great at leading discussions. So, I need to ask our IT team about indexing because that could solve some immediate issues," I said.

"If the data is not indexed properly, indexing could help, but if you have had a data integrity problem in the past, you will have a little more work."

"What do you mean?" I asked.

"Have you ever had a situation where the financials are produced, you report the numbers, and a day later, you find out they were wrong?"

"Oh my God, that happened to us last year. It was not pretty. I was told one of the source systems didn't update properly. I blew a gasket," I explained, putting my hands on my head.

"What did you do after that?"

"I told the CFO that I wanted his team to manually validate all the data before we report numbers."

"So, you didn't trust the data?" she asked.

"Hell no."

"Then you have a data integrity problem. It's been my experience that there is only one way to solve a data integrity problem."

"What's that? Just double-check the process?"

"Of course, you have to double-check and find out what is broken. But in your situation, I am sure they fixed it right?"

"They said it's fixed," I said.

"Do you still have finance double-check the numbers manually?"

"Yes. I can't afford for that to happen again."

"Have you had a problem since?"

"No."

"But you still don't trust the data?"

"No," I said, looking down.

"Then your data has a public relations problem," Ally said. "The only solution to a PR problem is to admit the problem. How can I explain this? Have you ever been to a restaurant and had a fabulous meal with your wife, and when you get home, you find yourself crippled over with food poisoning? You are up all night, and you think you are going to die."

"Yes, once at a Mexican restaurant."

"What did you do the next morning?"

"I told everyone I know to never go there!"

"Did you call the restaurant and tell them you were sick?"

"No."

"Then you handled it like your business teams are handling bad data. If they have gotten sick on the data in the past, they may not say anything. Instead, they will dump the data into Excel and do their own analysis. Unfortunately, they don't always dump the right data. Think about how many hours are wasted on what I call 'data chasing and manual analysis.' I'm curious. What if you had called the restaurant and they offered you and your wife a free meal with drinks? Would you go back?"

"No way," I said.

"What's the one thing that would get you to go back into the restaurant?" Ally asked.

"Probably nothing," I laughed.

"What if you drove by and there was a large sign out front that said 'under new management?' Would you consider going in?"

"Maybe."

"I believe data integrity problems need to be addressed the same way. When you fix the data issues, you need to post an 'under new management' sign. The way you do this is to first have the IT team members announce that they know they have a problem and they need the business's help to solve it. Then, invite the business users to share their ideas on how they need to use the data and discuss the problems they have had in the past. Ask for the users' ideas on how to fix the problem, and create a plan to fix it. The business should be informed and consulted as progress is made. This 'under new management' process increases the likelihood that end users will come back and use the system."

"Hold on," I said. "I need to start taking notes. You have given me so many great ideas. What I am hearing is that our real issues are with communication and partnering. That doesn't sound like it will cost us a ton to fix. But I am not sure my IT team has the facilitation and soft skills to pull this off."

"No problem. That's my specialty," said Ally as she tossed her long hair back over her shoulder. "So, how are we doing? Are you feeling more comfortable? Any questions so far?"

"This is excellent. I feel like this is actually manageable. But can you explain that closed loop solution a little more? I am confused by the difference between BI and analytics. And what's predictive versus prescriptive?"

"Sure," Ally said as she began drawing a box with a colorful pie chart and a bar graph. Then, she drew an arrow going from the data mart and added 'data warehouse' to the box.

"This is the BI tool. A good tool will allow for bursting of reports and dashboards. Dashboards are visualized views of the data that users can interact with. The key to a good dashboard is the information must be *actionable*, meaning if sales are decreasing, your people can take action to solve it. A dashboard should allow the users to drill to the appropriate details to find out the root cause of the problem. Ultimately, you want a BI tool that will allow users to create their own dashboards under a self-service model. But that should not be rolled out until you fix the data issues. It also typically requires a cultural shift where the end users are excited and are trained to understand the data."

Then, Ally drew another box where she labeled 'forecasting/ planning' with arrows going bi-directionally between the 'BI' box, the 'forecasting' box, and the 'data warehouse' box.

"I am a big believer that your budgets, forecasts, and planning should be part of the business intelligence infrastructure. Your forecasts will pull data from data marts or the warehouse. This includes data like actuals that are staged in the warehouse from your ledger. If the data is already in a data package in your BI tool, you could just get it from there. But the forecast should have the latest actuals for comparison. Then, your teams should update the forecast in a flexible budget and planning tool. Ideally, that updated forecast will automatically feed your BI reports so you can view the forecasts with actual comparisons. Personally, I think that budgets are outdated and that every company should be doing a rolling forecast, but that's a whole different discussion," she said with a smile.

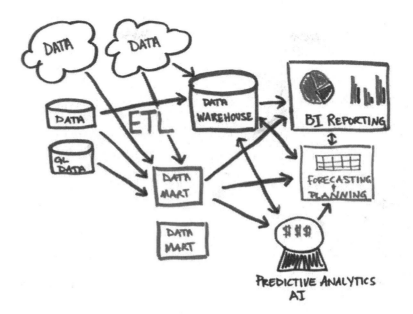

Ally proceeded to draw what looked like a crystal ball at the bottom of the page and then drew an arrow coming from the data marts to the object. "Is that a crystal ball?" I asked.

"Why, yes, it is," she giggled. "That is where we have our predictive and prescriptive analytics. Predictive analytics forecasts potential future outcomes based on data, whereas prescriptive analytics helps make recommendations based on the data. Both involve using machines to do the work to analyze millions of records. When people talk about artificial intelligence, they are basically saying, 'let the machines do the work.' You see, analytics is just using math and algorithms to gain insight from the data and, ideally, adding visualizations so laypeople can understand it.

"Have you heard the term 'descriptive analytics?' It's just taking the numbers to calculate something that describes the data, like the average temperature or the average cost of gas. Predictive analytics can be confusing because people assume it's used for forecasting, which it can be but not always. Another term used for predictive is 'advanced analytics.' With advanced analytics, math doesn't just describe the data but helps us understand the relationship between the data. For example, when the temperature is 10 degrees higher in the summer in the US, sunscreen sales will increase 10%, and waterpark admissions will be up 21%. See, it's the relationship."

"Well that seems simple enough. So, in theory, I could use predictive or advanced analytics to spot seasonality trends by letting the machine analyze my inventory and order histories. Then, it could recommend purchasing quantities and schedules to optimize my purchasing. Right?" My brain was spinning. I had been avoiding getting into the weeds with regard to our purchasing and had left it up to the department heads, but I suspect we could save a lot of money by controlling our inventory better.

"That's exactly it!" Ally said with a huge smile. "Another place distributors use predictive analytics is to deal with the always-uncomfortable discussion around customer credit. If you have the historical data, you can use predictive analytics on the CRM data and accounts receivables to monitor customers. Most companies establish credit for the customer based on the outside credit agencies' ratings, like TransUnion, when the customer was initially set up. Many companies don't review their clients' credit again until there's an issue. Predictive analytics models can examine the history of customers that have gone bad and identify the warning signs. The machine might learn that an increasing delay in customers returning phone calls is a warning sign. People don't like to call creditors back when they don't have money to pay their bills. In the future, when the machine examines the CRM data with the accounts receivable data, it could present an alert of clients that might have credit issues earlier, saving a distributor a ton in bad debt."

"You know, a couple years ago, we had a couple of clients who went bankrupt. We took a big hit. Do we need to hire a data scientist to do predictive analytics? I hear they are expensive and that it is hard to find good ones."

"You could hire a data scientist, and if you want, I know some good ones who are contractors I could connect you with. But with the advancement in the tools today, a subject matter expert that has some analytic aptitude can become what Gartner coined a 'citizen data scientist.' According to Gartner, a leading research and advisory company, a citizen data scientist is a person who creates or generates models that use advanced diagnostic analytics or predictive and prescriptive capabilities but whose primary job function is outside the field of statistics and analytics."[4]

"So many terms to remember," I said. "So, a citizen data scientist is a smart subject matter expert who learns to do analytics?"

"Pretty much. You may want to hire a data scientist at least on a project basis to lead your team in the right direction and for advanced needs. I know it gets confusing, even for those of us in the industry. Gartner also coined another new term, 'augmented analytics,' which is basically an approach that automates insights by using machine learning and natural language to automate the data preparation so information can be used by operational workers and data citizens. This doesn't eliminate the need for a data scientist entirely, but its goal is to bring advanced analytics to the masses."

"What's natural language generation?"

"Oh, sorry. Natural language generation is when the machine converts what it discovers into language or words. For example, if a customer reached his or her credit limit, the machine could convert the data point into a letter or email alerting the client and the sales representative in charge of the situation."

"Okay, so I get what natural language generation is, but you lost me on augmented analytics. What is it?"

"Let me back up. What you say about data scientists is true. Good ones can be expensive but if they discover relationship that could save or make the company a million dollars annually, it's probably worth the expense. A challenge can be that the data scientists may not have a strong understanding of the business. Therefore, executives must spend a lot of time with the data scientists to make sure the analytics make sense for the business. What we find is that data scientists spend a lot of time cleaning your garage," Ally laughed. "Maybe 80% of their time is spent cleaning, labeling, and validating data. Data chasing. So, what augmented analytics does is reduce the reliance on data scientists. The augmenting analytics engine can go through your data, clean it, analyze it, and convert insights into actionable steps."

"Isn't that what tools like SaS and Tableau do? I remember in the demo they said they 'support' analysis."

"Wow, look at you, Mr. I-don't-know-anything," Ally flipped her hair again. "Yes, those tools support analysis by simplifying the communication of the results, but they don't do the data clean-up, and to understand all the relationships in the data, you still need a data scientist or at least a business analyst. The challenge augmented analysis is trying to solve is getting data and analytics out to the masses. It's designed to deliver useful predictive information to your non-analytically minded team members. It does this by preparing the data, conducting the analysis, and generating business insights automatically with little to no supervision. Your whole team can use it. Some argue augmented analytics is the future of analytics."

My hand started to hurt from all the notes I had taken. I dropped the pen and began to massage my hand. "Man, I haven't taken that many notes since college." I smiled.

"Ally, I can't thank you enough. I feel so, so enlightened! I am still a little uncertain of how to become successful, but I have no doubt you know your stuff."

"Well, I don't know everything. My clients like me because I am highly connected. When I don't know an answer, I will know someone who does," explained Ally.

I looked down at my watch. We were almost to San Diego. "Ally, are you based in Tampa?"

"Yes, most of the year," she said, flashing her flirtatious smile again.

"Great. I want to talk to my executive team. I want to bring you in to help us. I hope you can squeeze me into your calendar. I have no doubt that you are in demand."

Ally blushed. "I've learned to be very selective in who I work with, James. I only work with companies I believe are committed to the process. But I get the impression that you are willing to do the work. I am at Brendon's High-Performance Academy until Sunday, and then, I'm heading out to Colorado to get a little skiing in, but I will be back next Thursday."

"Perfect, how about we connect then? Maybe you could stop by our office and meet the executive team."

"Sure, but you don't get off that easily," Ally said as she picked up my pen and handed it to me. "I give everyone homework. You're going to have to write this down. Your homework is to go to our website and download our BI Action Assessment Indicator. I want you to give the form to each of your executives and ask them to answer open and honestly. When you get them back, have your assistant send them to me. I will need them no later than Tuesday night so I can review them before we meet on Thursday. I'll also send you our standard NDA and contract terms so we can discuss that on Thursday. The last thing you must do is document your strategic goals and how you measure them. If you already have them, just send them to me. If not, you and your executive team will have some work to do," she said, smiling. "James, I am excited to the have the opportunity to work with you. I hope your team is like you."

Ally bent over to reach her bag, pulling out a business card and handing it to me with the picture of business intelligence she had drawn. I handed her a card from my coat pocket. "Oh, wait," she said, pulling the picture back. She scribbled her signature. "That will be worth a lot when I am famous," she laughed.

A complete sense of peace overwhelmed me. I started thinking about ways we could leverage data. Could Ally be correct? Was communication the root of our problem? I hoped so.

Once we landed and deplaned, I said, "Ally, I can't thank you enough. This has been the best flight all year. I am so inspired! Can I give you a hug?"

"Sure," Ally said, standing on her tippy toes as we embraced. As we let go, she said, "I want to leave you with one comment as we part ways: If you don't take the time and energy to do business intelligence correctly, what will happen if your competitors do? She gave one last sassy smile and scurried down the terminal.

Key Takeaways:

- To be an analytic leader, you must first start by understanding the terminology and basics.
- The definitions in disparate systems need to be standardized for reporting.
- IT protects the data. Business owns the data.
- A data mart is a subset or small data warehouse.
- An enterprise data warehouse can stage the data with standardized definitions for BI.
- The MacGyver approach is where you define the most important situation that will positively impact the bottom line and you solve it rapidly, delivering a minimal viable product.
- ETL stands for "extract, transform, and load."
- Lack of indexing is a common reason users are frustrated with reporting.
- Requirements need to be discovered. They can't be gathered.
- Data integrity problems need to be addressed by using an "under new management" sign.

- Analytics leverages math and algorithms to gain insight from the data and ideally adds visualizations so laypeople can understand it.

- With advanced analytics, math doesn't just describe the data but helps us understand the relationship between the data.

- Natural language generation is when the machine converts what it discovers into language or words.

- An augmented analytics engine can go through your data, clean it, analyze it, and convert insights into actionable steps.

- If you don't take the time and energy to do business intelligence correctly, what will happen if your competitors do?

Heatherized

Wow, you are doing fabulous! You should have learned a lot in that last section, and have a good basic understanding of the components of business intelligence. Your peers will be impressed with your knowledge. Keep up the great work. I am committed to guiding you to lead your organization through the data revolution and transforming it with data and analytics.

If you haven't downloaded the supplemental tools, please do so now. Simply register at www.Heatherized.com/bookbonus, and you will gain access to many tools to aid you in your journey to become an analytic leader!

Here is what you'll receive:

- BI Action Assessment Indicator
- Core Values worksheet
- Questionnaires
- Sample job description for attracting BI superstars
- Videos to improve communication and provide time-saving methods
- And more!

Sign up today at www.Heatherized.com/BookBonus.

CHAPTER 4

Executive Buy-In

"A leader takes people where they want to go. A great leader takes people where they don't necessarily want to go, but ought to be."

–Rosalynn Carter

I walked into The Coffee Cup, a quaint little coffee shop hidden in the Gaslamp District. I had some time before my next meeting, and I needed to get caught up on email. The rich coffee smell engulfed me as I entered. The reclaimed wood floors and dark red walls gave it a cozy feel. It was the perfect place to focus. I ordered a latte and found a small table in the corner by the window. I booted up my laptop and found the Wi-Fi, named CoffeeCup. Dang, I forgot to get the password. I looked around, but it wasn't posted.

"Excuse me," I said to the young man working on his computer at the table next to me. He looked like a regular. "Do you happen to know the password to the Wi-Fi?"

"Sure, it's Drinkupandorderanother, only the D is capital, and there are no spaces," he said, not even looking up.

"Thanks."

I logged on, and there in my email was an message from Ally.

James,

It was a pleasure to meet you this morning. As you can tell, I love talking about Faster Cheaper Analytics to anyone who will listen. Here's a link to where you can download the BI Action Assessment Indicator.

www.Heatherized.com/BIAction

Please have each of your executive team members complete this and send me the results before we meet on Thursday. Would 9 a.m. at your office work for a meeting with you and your team? If so, I'll send you a meeting invite. Our goal of the meeting is to provide an overview of what we talked about for your team.

You mentioned that you want to get started right away. If you would like to get started with the Executive Buy- In section of the program, we could start with a one-day session on Thursday. To make this happen, we would need to execute the NDA and contract for the initial one-day session. After this session, we can both evaluate our relationship and determine if we both want to move forward. As I stated, I only work with clients I feel are committed to the transformation. To start Thursday, you would need to ensure that all your executives are available and can be completely present. So, they need to clear their calendars completely. I have attached the necessary paperwork for your review and signature.

I look forward to working with you.

Ally

Wow, she is on the ball. I forwarded the email to my executive team with a note briefly describing my encounter with Ally. I included Ally's last comment, "If we don't take the time and energy to do business intelligence correctly, what will happen if our competitors do?" I then asked them to clear their calendars for a week from Thursday. I was overcome by nervous excitement. It's that feeling I get when I know something great is about to happen. I felt it in my fingertips. I forwarded the contracts to legal with a note that they were top priority and I needed them by a week from Wednesday at the latest.

The week flew by quickly. It was the big day, and we were meeting with Ally at 9 a.m. I was like a child on Christmas morning. I got up earlier than normal. Mary, my wife, handed me a cup of coffee and joked, "What's up with you? You have a new spring in your step."

"No," I responded. "I am just really excited. Remember I told you about the woman I met on the flight to San Diego, the Business Analytics Advisor, Ally?"

"Yes," she said with a raised eyebrow.

"Well, today, she's coming in to inspire the executive team and help us create a roadmap so we can succeed at business intelligence and analytics. I really believe this is going to be game-changing for us. The more I think about it, the more strongly I feel that we can gain back market share and increase our profits, leaving our competition in the dust," I said, almost popping out of my chair.

"Well," she said with a smile, "I love seeing you like this. You haven't been this excited about work in years. But you might want to go for a run because the way you're acting right now, you won't be able to sit still in a meeting," she laughed, noticing my leg shaking.

Mary was right. Butterflies were dancing in my stomach, and the nervous excitement was overwhelming. A quick early morning run on Bayshore would calm me down.

During the run, I couldn't stop thinking about how crazy it was that the coincidental meeting of Ally on a plane could lead to organizational transformation. Hmm, probably not a coincidence.

I've always believed everything happens for a reason. If we could get the executive team on board and excited, that could energize the entire company. Sure, we might lose people who don't believe in the vision, but my initial research showed that our competitors were struggling with data and analytics transformation as well. We could be the first.

"No, we will be the first," I thought. How amazing would it be to be the company all the others admired? The excitement of this opportunity made work fun again. Yes, it will be a lot of work, but I've always loved a challenge. It's funny. Just two weeks ago, I was in a funk, bored with my life. I felt like I was in a rut and couldn't wait to retire.

———————

Sarah greeted me with a cup of coffee as I walked into the office. I gave her a big smile that caught her off guard.

"Wow, you seem like you are in a good mood," she said.

"I am. Today is a big day. It could even be game-changing. You did reserve the Chicago conference room, right, Sarah?" I asked.

"Yes, and Ally Canfield showed up early. She is already in the room. She said she needed to set up."

I strolled into my office to quickly check email and turn my out-of-office notice on, thinking, "I wonder what she had to set up." I had a feeling this was not going to be our typical boring meeting.

A few minutes later, I headed to the Chicago conference room. "Good morning, Ally," I said. "Did Sarah offer you coffee?"

"Yes, I am all set. Thanks," she said, raising her cup. "I just needed to get set up." I looked around the room and saw three easels with flip charts on them scattered around the room. On the whiteboard, she had written a big "32." On the floor beside Ally was a large brown box, but I couldn't tell what was in it.

"I hope you guys are ready to have some fun. I think we need a little inspiration," she said as she flashed a big smile, plugged her iPhone into the sound system, and played "It's a Great Day to Be Alive" by Travis Tritt.

As the others entered the room, they looked a little shocked. "Are we in the right place?" Chris asked.

I laughed and said, "Yes, gentlemen. I would like to introduce you to our Business Analytics Advisor, Ally Canfield. Ally, this is Chris, our CFO, Bob, our CIO, Steve, our CMO, and Mark, our COO. We are just waiting for Susan, our CHRO."

"It's a pleasure to meet you," Ally shook everyone's hands and then handed each of us a string of colorful beads. "Please put the beads on, and I'll explain later how we will use them," she said, flashing her bright smile. "We have a few minutes before our 9 o'clock start time. So, if you could please turn your out-of-office messages on if you haven't already. We need everyone 100% present today. I will give you set breaks to check for any emergencies. If you need coffee or water, please get it now," Ally said as she looked at the clock. It was 8:55 a.m. "We will start in five minutes sharp."

At precisely 9 a.m., Ally turned off the music and said, "Welcome! Please be seated. I want to congratulate you on taking the first step to becoming an analytic leader! I am Ally Canfield, your Business Analytics Advisor. I am super excited to be here today and hope you are too. My goal is to help you become analytic leaders and teach you how to increase your market share and transform your organization to be data and analytics-driven. James tells me you are struggling a bit but that you guys are willing to explore new methods." I looked around the room, and people were nodding slightly.

"Before we get started, let me share my background. I've been in some form of the data and analytics space for over 25 years. Yes, I literally grew up with it, as my parents had a software company. My background is finance, IT, and law, so I am highly analytical, which is a gift and curse. I am also a certified high-performance coach. As we work together, I will teach you and your teams methods to increase productivity and reduce your stress. How many of you feel you don't have enough hours in the day?" We all raised our hands.

"Well, I will teach you to gain control of your time. Too many companies claim they fail at BI because they don't have enough resources, especially time, so we will address that quickly. The best way to save time is not to waste it."

"Should we wait for Susan?" I interrupted Ally.

"No, sorry," Ally said. "One of the ground rules for our meetings is that we start on time and end on time. If we don't, we will waste time. My mother always told me if you show up just on time, you are late. She said it was a form of respect. Think about how much time is wasted in meetings because people are late. So, we will start on time. If you aren't here, we will proceed without you. Can everyone agree to that?" We all nodded. She's right. So much time is wasted with people showing up late.

"Great. The next rule is that we are 100% present. That means cell phones are on airplane mode, laptops are put away unless needed, and we all are focused. I find this can cut meeting times down significantly. Can everyone agree to that?" We nodded again.

Ally removed the cover of the projector. There was a picture of a tree with a yellow weathered sign that had an arrow pointing left under the word "easy" and an arrow pointing right under the word "difficult."

"You have a choice," Ally said. You can choose the easy way to do business intelligence and analytics, or you can choose the difficult way. Most companies struggle with business intelligence, data, and analytics and choose the difficult way because they don't know how to go the easy way. My goal is to coach you on how to take the easy path.

The door opened, and Susan walked in. "Sorry I am late," she said, grabbing a seat in the back. Ally nodded in Susan's direction but continued.

"There are a few more rules of engagement." Ally advanced to the next slide and read the rules out loud.

- We start on time.
- We will be 100% present (no phones or email).
- We are here to learn.
  - We don't know everything, and that's okay!
- We will bring positive attitudes into this room.
  - If you are having a bad day, consider the door frame a portal. As you pass through it, you change your mindset to be positive.
- We will fail and fail fast.
  - Failure is celebrated as long as we learned something from it and do it quickly. U-turns are okay.
- We will agree to play full out!!!
- This is a safe space for crazy ideas.
  - Crazy ideas lead to disruption and innovation.
- The word "but" is not allowed.

"'But' is a negative word. It's a blocker," Ally said. "Each of you has a string of beads on." Ally grabbed a purple string from the table and walked it over to Susan.

"The beads are for a game we will play called the 'No Buts' game. For the rest of the day, you are not allowed to say the word 'but'—either form of it," she smiled. "If you say the word 'but' and someone catches you, the first person to call it out will take all your beads. At the end of the day, we will have a little prize for the person with the most beads. The reason we play this game is that I have found that in companies, it's easy to say why something will not work or to limit an idea before it gets going. We hear, but we don't have resources. But we don't have data... So, I am going to challenge you to think differently. Let me give you an example, and then we will officially start the game. Let's say I wanted to build a dashboard that showed late deliveries and wanted to drill down to the reason they were late. Bob might say, 'But we don't have that data.'"

Bob nodded. "You're right. We don't capture that data."

"By saying *but* we don't have the data, Bob is essentially killing the idea." We nodded. "What if, instead, Bob said, 'Yes, a deliveries dashboard would be great, and this would be an opportunity to evaluate what data we are capturing so we can provide the details you desire'? We call this a '*yes and.*' Do you see the difference? We turned a 'but' into a positive opportunity by using '*yes and*' instead."

I looked around the room, and everyone was smiling. She was right. It created a completely different atmosphere.

"Okay, the game is officially beginning. Now that we have the ground rules, are we all comfortable with the rules? Can we agree to abide by them? We nodded, and Ally grabbed a small stack of papers and handed one to each of us. "Great. Then you won't mind signing the agreement," she said.

I was shocked. Did she really want us to sign a contract?

Ally laughed. "You guys look a little surprised. Yes, I want you to sign the sheets because you are committing to each other that this is important and that you respect this opportunity and each other. I have found that when people sign things, they honor the agreement more."

Interesting. "She's probably right," I thought, and I signed the document and handed it back to her. The others did as well.

"Fabulous. Now that we have the administrative stuff done, I want to share with you your BI Action Assessment Indicator results. Each of you completed a short questionnaire in which you scored where you thought your organization was in different categories: people, processes, tools, and data. The 10 questions are designed to make you think. How do you think you guys did?"

"It was eye-opening," said Steve. "I knew we were struggling with BI because in marketing, we do a lot of manual analysis in Excel. But the questions made me really realize that we were setting ourselves up for failure."

"I don't think I scored anything over a four," said Susan as she raised her eyebrows.

"It made me realize we have a lot of room to improve," Mark said.

"You are absolutely correct, Mark. You can only get better." Ally grinned while gritting her teeth. "I averaged your scores, and your average organizational score that you gave yourselves is 32 out of 100. The highest-scoring category was tools with a 43. Your lowest category was end user adoption. Does anyone have any comments on this?"

"I found the assessment eye-opening. I think there are things we can start doing now that would affect the people and processes sections immediately. Although we scored really low, I am optimistic that we can dramatically change our score," I said. I looked around the room and found a few people nodding.

"The score is higher than I thought it would be," Bob proclaimed. Everyone chuckled.

"Well, the good news is that I am confident we can get your number a lot higher," Ally grinned. "Clearly, we have some work to do, so let's get started." She handed each of us a stack of sticky notes.

"I want to introduce you to the power of the sticky note. You will find we use a lot of them. They are fabulous for brainstorming and prioritizing. What you will do is write down what you want to get out of today. What do you want to cover, learn, and discuss? For example, I want to better understand your strategic goals, so I would write 'review strategic goals' on one sticky note. Please write only one idea per sticky note. I will set the timer, and you will only have three minutes. Any questions?" She peered around the room. "Okay, start now."

A rush came over me. I felt like I was in fourth grade again, taking a timed math test. I wanted to be done first. I wrote down a few points on the notes. I looked around, and the others were writing rapidly. At three minutes, Ally's phone buzzed.

"Time's up," Ally said as she pulled a small stack of sticky notes out of her notebook. "Before we get started on your ideas, I want to share with you something that completely changed my life. This is a technique that made me so much more productive. It can be game-changing for you and your teams. It's called time blocking. You've already experienced it. Did you notice how focused you were writing down your ideas? That's the magic of time blocking," Ally grinned.

"Let me give you an example you can probably relate to. Let's say I had all day Saturday to clean my house. How long do you think it would take me?"

"All day," I said.

"Exactly, and I might not even get it done," she laughed. "However, what would happen if I received a text message from a friend that said, 'Hey, I am going to swing by your house. See you in an hour'?" We sat in silence for a moment, all reflecting on an experience where unexpected guests arrived.

"I would start cleaning like a madwoman, right? I'd be running around my house, throwing stuff in closets. Do not look under my bed. How many of you have been there?" Ally asked with a goofy smile.

We all start laughing. Susan said, "That happened to me last week."

"Yes, it's amazing what you can accomplish when you have limited time. That's the secret behind time blocking. By setting a timer, we stop daydreaming and focus. I believe this one technique has doubled my productivity. Here's how it works: When I have a project or task, I put it on my calendar as 'do not disturb.' I set a timer and put my phone on airplane mode. I do not allow myself to check email, Facebook, LinkedIn, or text messages. I stay completely focused and crank it out. When I time block, I do it in blocks that are no more than 50 minutes. Studies have proven that you need to get up and walk around or get water and take a break every 50 minutes to maximize productivity. Do you think you could try implementing that in your life and meetings?"

I started to think about how many projects I started and stopped due to distractions. How I used frivolous things as a distraction when

I wanted to procrastinate. This simple technique is definitely worth trying. I nodded my head.

"Okay, who would like to start sharing their ideas about what they want to cover today?" she asked.

"I will," I said.

"Perfect. James, what I want you to do is briefly introduce yourself and tell me how you're feeling right now. Tell us how you are feeling by giving us a score from zero to 10, zero being 'just shoot me now,' and 10 being 'I feel amazing.' Then, give one word to describe how you are feeling. Finally, share each item you have on your notes. For the rest of you, if you have the same item, please just pull the duplicates from your pile."

I said, "Hi, I am James Brown, CEO, and my number is an eight. Hmm, a word... It would have to be either 'inspired' or 'curious.'"

"Great," said Ally. "What would make your number higher so we can move you to a nine?"

"I guess if I knew more about what's about to happen, that might move me up, but I feel pretty good," I said.

Mark blurted out, "You said it. Give me your beads." Everyone laughed, and I handed Mark my beads. Mark put them over his head with pride.

"Well done," said Ally, clapping her hands. "Clearly, you were listening. Okay. James, please share your items. At this point, we will not debate them. We just want to create a master list, so you can place them on the flip chart over there."

I went through my list.

- How much will this cost?
- Review the strategic goals & how we measure them
- Understand why you wanted our strategic goal
- Understand why we have failed at BI in the past
- Understand where we can get quick wins
- What do we have to do differently?

- What resources will we need? Time, people, consultants?
- Understand what commitment you need from the executive team
- What results we can expect if we engage you

"That's a fabulous list. Do you have any more?"

"No, that's about it."

"Okay, who's next?"

Bob raised his hand and said, "Okay, I'm Bob. I have, 'How do we deal with data when we don't have a data warehouse?"

"Bob, can you please provide us with your number reflecting how you are feeling and a word?"

"Oh yeah, sorry. I am at about a six. I think my word would be 'anxious.' To get to a higher number, I would need to have fewer fires burning at my desk," Bob smiled halfheartedly.

"Fair enough. I think we can all relate to that," Ally said. "Please share the rest of your items."

The remaining team members each shared their numbers, what would make them higher, a word, and their items.

"Well, it looks like we have a fabulous list here. As you can imagine, we will not be able to cover all of these today due to lack of time, but we now know what everyone's expectations are. I do have one item I want to add to the list, and that's how to get quick wins that affect the bottom line with business intelligence. I call this the MacGyver approach." Ally placed her note on the flip chart and flashed me her energized smile. I had tried to explain the MacGyver approach to the team when I told them about meeting Ally, but I was glad she added it to the agenda.

"Why did you ask us for a number and a word?" asked Susan.

"Well, I can better communicate with you when I know how you are feeling. If you are stressed like Bob is, I will understand if his comments are a little curt. Think about it. When you need to talk to your spouse about something sensitive, don't you first get a read on their mood?"

"I love that," Susan said, scribbling notes in her journal. "What a great idea."

"Okay, let's play another game," Ally said. "Who would like to volunteer?" Ally looked directly at Chris, almost forcing him to raise his hand.

"I guess I will," he said as everyone laughed.

"Please come to the front of the room." Chris walked up, not sure what to expect. "Do you mind if I blindfold you?" Ally asked.

"Ah, I guess not," Chris said a little uneasily.

"Okay, close your eyes." As Chris closed his eyes, Ally pulled out a hot pink blindfold with hearts on it and wrapped it around Chris's head. Everyone laughed. "What?" Chris asked.

"Oh, nothing," Ally said in a sweet, sassy voice. "I need another volunteer." No one offered for fear of being blindfolded. "Susan, do you mind helping me out? I promise I won't blindfold you," Ally said, waving Susan to the front.

"Sure," Susan said as she stood up.

"Chris, you can't see anything, right?"

"No, nothing," Chris replied.

"Good." Ally reached into the large box on the floor and pulled out a dartboard. I wondered what the heck was she planning.

"Susan, could you please hold this? But do not say a word." Susan grabbed the dartboard with an apprehensive smile. Ally took Susan's hand and led her to the left side of the room, about 10 feet from Chris. "Chris, are you ready?"

"Um, I guess."

"Okay, I am going to hand you magnetic darts. Your job is to throw them at the dartboard that Susan is holding. Each dart represents a dashboard for a different department or initiative. Ally handed Chris a blue dart. This will represent a finance dashboard. Now, I'll give you a hint. Susan is not right in front of you," Ally giggled.

"Can you give me a hint about which direction I should throw?"

"What do you mean? I just did. I said she wasn't in front of you." Chris rotated 45 degrees to his left and threw the dart. It sailed in the opposite direction from where Susan was standing. We laughed as it bounced off the floor.

"Sorry, Chris. You missed. How do you feel right now?"

"I'm a two, and my word is 'frustrated.'" We laughed again, which made Chris laugh.

"Okay, Chris, we will let you try again. But this time, Susan will say the word "bull's-eye" to give you a clue where she is. Do you think that will help?"

"Yes."

"Susan."

"Bull's-eye," Susan sang out.

Chris spun around, now facing about 20 degrees right of Mary, and tossed the second dart in the air. Susan looked relieved, as she didn't want to get hit in the head.

"Wow, so much closer. It's not quite delivering the dashboard HR was looking for, however. Let's try this one more time. This dart represents operations," she said, handing him a dart. "But this time, I will remove your blindfold." Ally untied the pink blindfold.

As Chris looked down, he noticed the color of the blindfold with the hearts and smiled. He looked around the room, noticing how far off his darts were. He then looked at Susan. Susan held the dartboard over her face. Chris tossed the dart, hitting the board directly in the center.

"Bull's-eye!" Ally cried out and clapped. "Well done. Thank you both for being great sports. Chris, how are you feeling now?"

"A 10, and my word is 'bull's-eye.'" He smiled back at Ally, who gave him a high five as he went to sit down.

"Okay, so you might be wondering what this has to do with delivering BI and analytics."

"Exactly," Mark said.

"Well, the first dart represented how you are delivering BI today. You are setting IT up for failure." Bob sat straighter in his chair, almost puffing out this chest.

"Your end users don't know what is possible with business intelligence and analytics, and IT can't read their minds—just like the first dart users are not providing visibility to IT as to what they want or need. IT is blindfolded. IT and the business users aren't communicating in the same language, so IT is guessing where to aim based on the limited information it has. You noticed when there's even a little communication, like when Susan said 'bull's-eye,' Chris got a lot closer. When IT is given visibility and there's two-way communication with the business users, IT can deliver a bull's-eye with business intelligence tools."

Ally then explained that most BI professionals don't know the strategic goals of their companies. I noticed everyone looked down as if they were guilty. She explained how IT and business users communicate differently and that members of IT need to improve their listening and facilitation skills.

"Bob, would you agree that your team is not set up for success?"

"Absolutely," Bob said, popping out of his chair and walking to the front of the room to look everyone in the eye.

"Guys, we want to deliver, but we can't do it without you. My team is great, but they don't have the business knowledge that your teams have. In the past, when we requested meetings with the various departments to gather requirements, some of you sent your interns to meet with us. Your interns barely know the business. But we need access to your rock stars and to you." Bob was more passionate than I've seen him years. I looked around the room, and the expressions were of understanding.

Ally placed her hand on Bob's shoulder. "Thank you, Bob. I can tell you are a great leader. However, I am afraid you need to give me your beads. You said the word." We laughed as Ally stripped Bob of his beads. "How about we take a break?"

The rest of the day, we covered most of the list we had put on the agenda flip chart. Ally explained the MacGyver approach, which everyone loved, especially Bob. We walked through our strategic goals and how we could measure them, confirming our Key Performance

Indicators (KPIs). We covered items like carrying cost of inventory, inventory turns, order pick accuracy, units per transaction, rate of return, inventory accuracy, backorder rate, and inventory-to-sales ratios. We were familiar with many of the KPIs but identified that we were not good at delivering the information to people who could act on them.

Ally walked us through the fundamentals and terminology of business intelligence, decoding all the analytics industry jargon that seems to make everyone feel comfortable. She guided everyone through the diagram that she had drawn for me on the plane and identified where companies usually had challenges. We all agreed to help IT clean up the data, which seemed to make Bob very happy.

Ally explained to the team that KPIs were great, but the real power was when we add a predictive component to the data. She explained that KPIs still offer a rearview mirror perspective of what happened. Yes, knowledgeable people with industry and business insights can act on the KPIs if they are trending in the wrong direction. However, when a firm uses predictive or advanced analytics where machines analyze millions of records of the data and the machine connects the dots to reveal relationships almost impossible for humans to find, that's game-changing. When we act on the machine's discoveries, we can dominate our competition.

As Ally explained this, Steve, the CMO, was bouncing with excitement. This meant he could target his marketing campaigns like a sniper rifle instead of doing the shotgun approach, as Ally calls it.

Ally then had each one of us brainstorm for 15 minutes with sticky notes about how we could leverage data and predictive analytics and what the results of having that information would be. She gave the example of predictive maintenance on our trucks. According to Ally, we could monitor the truck's usage and the current status of the vehicle's various key components and then have the predictive tools to plan a preventive maintenance schedule. Basically, the data would predict component failure while a truck was on the road or in the shop. This could save us millions in down time, spoiled goods, and dissatisfied customers, not to mention reducing the stress of drivers, customers, and sales reps. I loved the idea of not having trucks break down. I wondered if we could use it to monitor driving patterns and calculate a risk factor for each driver on the likelihood of them getting into an accident. Or, maybe, it could connect with Google Maps or something and recommend a better route for the drivers to take when road construction was happening. My head was racing.

Ally explained that the crazier an idea was, the better. It did not matter if it was feasible today or if we currently had the data. We were to let our minds wander. Find your inner Elon Musk, as she called it. She set the timer, and we all wrote frantically. The ideas we came up with in just 15 minutes were amazing.

"Good ideas are always crazy until they are not."

–Larry Page

After everyone presented their ideas and put them on the flip chart, Ally applauded and said, "Guys, these ideas are incredible! Now, we must do a high-level prioritization. Since we are a small group, we will do it all together. Here's how this works. I will read off one of the ideas and then a second idea. As a group, we will need to decide if the second idea is better than the first. Then, I'll read a third idea, and we will compare it to the first and second so we can define the order. If we start to have challenges and can't agree, then I'll give each of you three stickers. You will put a sticker on the three ideas you like the most. This allows us to focus on the ideas with the most stickers. Does that make sense?"

Wow, this was such a simple approach for getting people to focus. I think we could use this approach in all our meetings. We nodded our heads.

"Before we decide the order, we want to consider a number of factors, such as:

- How will it impact the bottom line?
- Do we have the data?
- How open to using data is the team or department it would serve?
- How rapidly could we deliver?

We have a limited amount of time, so we will not be debating these heavily. We only have 15 minutes to organize them," Ally said as she set the timer. "The goal is to just narrow our list down, and we will do more analysis on the top ideas later."

She began reading off the ideas, and the group really jelled together. After five minutes, Ally said, "We only have 10 more minutes. We need to keep moving. Do we agree this idea is more important that the last?"

She really held us to our time schedule. Everyone knew she would not let us extend the time. I was feeling so accomplished. We had done more in that day than we had in months of meetings. We weren't fighting or pointing fingers at was at fault for our failed BI. We were collaborating.

When we finished organizing our list, Ally said, "Look at that! We have 17 seconds left. Well done." She clapped her hands, and we all joined in. As she finished clapping, she said, "How do you guys feel? Bob?"

With a big grin, Bob said, "I think I'm at a nine. 'Excited' would be my word because I feel like I can focus my team on our priorities and really add value."

"Fabulous," Ally said, flashing her sassy smile. "Susan?"

"I am at a 9.5," Susan said. "'Inspired' would be the word. I see how HR could use your methods to teach everyone how to run effective meetings." Ally beamed. The rest of the team all had nines.

"Well, we need to celebrate!" Ally pulled out a box of beautifully decorated cupcakes. "You see, one thing people forget to do when they run projects is celebrate what they accomplish! It's the celebration and reflection of how awesome you worked as a team that keeps people motivated during the long projects." She handed each of us a cupcake and a napkin.

I felt like I was back in second grade when Ms. Anderson gave the class treats for scoring high on a quiz. I hadn't felt this proud in a long time.

"Well, enjoy your cupcakes, and then, I'll review how the rest of the process works, assuming that you guys want to continue working with me," Ally said with an inquisitive but confident look on her face.

"I think I can speak for the team, Ally," I said, wiping the frosting from my lip. "We would love to work with you. Right, guys?"

"Absolutely," Bob said.

We enjoyed our cupcakes and a brief break. When we returned, Ally said, "I have three things we need to cover, and we will then call it a day. First, we will talk about expectations. I believe expectations are a simple way to help reduce stress in our lives. Studies show that people who are less stressed and happier are more productive. Then, I will outline the rest of the BI Bull's-eye methodology, but remember, everything is flexible, so this is just a guideline. We can customize it for your specific needs. And finally, we will do one more brainstorming session exploring the cost of not moving forward. Does that work?" We all nodded.

"Okay, expectations. How many of you were disappointed in the last 24 hours? Maybe an employee let you down, maybe a family member? Maybe you got stuck in traffic when you normally don't?" We all raised our hands. "Kind of sucks, right? What if I could teach you a simple technique that would make it so you and the people in your life are not disappointed? Bob, how do your team members feel when they work hard on a dashboard and the end users don't use it?"

"Disappointed," Bob said.

"And Steve, how do you feel when Bob's team delivers a dashboard that doesn't do what you thought it was going to do?"

"Disappointed," said Steve.

"Bob, how would your team members feel if they delivered a dashboard the user loved?"

"I think my team members would feel pride. They would love that. Heck, it might help with our attrition issue," he said, looking at Susan.

"Well, here's a secret to a happy life! When I tell you, you must promise to share it with everyone. This is a key to the cultural transformation we are trying to achieve with data and analytics, so this is really important. Can you promise me you will share it with your team?"

"Yes!" we exclaimed.

"The secret is setting expectations. Yes, it's that simple. Think about it. There is only one reason anyone is disappointed. Yep, just one reason: their expectations were not met or exceeded. Think about it. James, I noticed Sarah greets you with coffee in the morning. What if one day, she didn't? What if the coffee maker broke?"

"I would be disappointed," I said.

"Why?"

"Because she has it ready for me every morning. I think she does it so I am not grumpy," I laughed, and so did the others.

"Yes, you would be disappointed and probably grumpy," Ally smiled. "But let's say before you arrived at the office, Sarah called you and told you the coffee maker broke and that she would not have coffee for you. Sarah suggests that you might want to grab a coffee on the way into the office. How would you feel?"

"Well, first, give me your beads. You said the word," I said, holding my hand out and smiling.

"Wow, you got me. Well done."

"I would feel a little disappointed that I had to make a trip to Dunkin Donuts for coffee; however, I would be glad she called me."

"Exactly. By calling, what Sarah is doing is reframing expectations. She can't fix the broken coffee maker, but she can communicate to you that expectations need to be updated."

"I have seen this one little technique of setting expectations change people's lives! I have a friend, Bill, who was completely stressed out. He hated his job and was thinking about changing careers. He said his clients were demanding and unrealistic, and it was getting worse. He had hired life coaches to help him transition. Over a drink one evening, I asked him if he would enjoy his work if his clients weren't so demanding and he controlled his schedule. He said he loved the work; it was the people he didn't like. I then challenged him like I am going to challenge you to start saying 'no' and to start reframing expectations. Bob, if your IT team is like most I work with, they are over-committed and stressed out."

"Yes," said Bob.

"When Chris or James calls your team and asks for information right away, what happens?"

"They drop everything and do it," said Bob with pride.

"Did you know that studies have proven that switching tasks or multitasking kills productivity? That's right. No one's brain is actually capable of multitasking. So, when Bob's team drops everything and switches projects, it takes a lot more time to complete the tasks. James, do you ever give advance notice of what you want, or is it always urgent?" Ally's eye twinkled in my direction.

"It's a mix, I would say."

"When you ask Bob's team members for something, do they ever ask you when you need the information?"

"Not usually," I thought. "No, I don't recall them asking that."

"If you were a mid-level IT person and the CEO called you and asked you for information, what would you do? Would you assume it's urgent?"

I remembered back in the day when I was trying to make my mark, I would have jumped through hoops for the CEO. "I guess I would try to get it to the CEO as fast as possible."

Bob looked down. "Yes, my guess is that my team assumes it's urgent, and they are eager to look good in front of him."

"What if, instead, we trained people to ask the person requesting the information what date they needed the information by? What if we trained them to double or triple their time estimate when people asked how long something would take? So, if they thought it would take a week, they say two to give IT some breathing room. James, would you be upset if IT told you they could get you the data in a week and then delivered it in three days?"

"No, I would be happy I got it early."

"Exactly. We need to train everyone to under-promise and over-deliver. The problem is that people fear saying 'no' or reframing expectations. So, this is something we need to coach them on to reduce stress and increase productivity." Susan was taking detailed notes.

"And what if, as executives, you acknowledged that people will jump through hoops for you, and you start communicating realistic deadlines? In other words, both sides reframe their expectations."

"Wow, that would be a huge stress reliever," Bob said.

"Gosh, I didn't realize I was part of the problem!" I blurted out. "My mind is now racing from how often I ask for stuff. Candidly, I usually don't even look at it until a few days before the board meeting, but I am given the information right away. I am going to work on setting better expectations immediately."

"Great. You see, if we as managers don't clearly articulate our expectations, our team will assume and fill in the blanks. The problem is that they are not good at reading your mind. So, they miss the mark, causing disappointment in you and them. Situations change, and when they do, you must reframe expectations. Even when expectations have to be adjusted, I recommend under-promising and over-delivering. Expectation setting is like a muscle. It takes repetitive practice! So, your homework is to start setting and reframing expectations 24/7."

I looked over at Susan, who was still vigorously taking notes. I needed to talk to her later about communicating this to everyone in the organization. Just having people set expectations and reframing when things change could be huge. Happy employees, fewer repeated tasks, satisfied managers...

"Do you think you could improve on how you communicate your expectations and reframe them?" Ally asked.

"Absolutely," we all responded. Ally beamed.

"Okay, now, I want to set expectations for the journey you are about to embark on." Ally tossed her long brown hair. "The first step is to understand how teams form and what skills and knowledge will help move your project along. As the executive team, you need to commit to each other to free up your superstars and not just assign a marketing intern," she said, smiling at Steve.

"So, we will have a discussion and define the talent. This may also require you to invest in some soft skill training for your team members. Am I correct in assuming your long-term goal is to deliver powerful data and analytics without reliance on expensive consultants?"

"Yes!" Bob and Chris shouted out.

"Then we will invite the larger team to what I call a 'foundations day.' We will follow the same ground rules in all our meetings—100% presence. In the foundations sessions, we will cover some of what you learned here today, like the industry jargon, and get everyone on the same page. We will also review the strategic goals and KPIs. We will make it fun, of course, with games. I like to use games I learned in improv class to help develop active listening skills."

"Improv class?" Susan asked.

"Yes, I took improv classes at Second City in Chicago, and I discovered improv can greatly improve IT professionals' soft skills. That's where the 'yes, and' concept comes from. Think about it. In improv, there's no script. You have no clue what the other people in your skit are going to do or say. It forces you to be completely present and listen instead of thinking about what brilliant thing you are going to say next. Personally, I think everyone should take an improv class, so we will do a few improv exercises with the team."

"Can't wait to see that," Bob said, laughing.

"Of course, we will introduce them to MacGyver, and we will evaluate the top items you came up with today along with the ideas they create. Bob, do you currently use an Agile or Scrum methodology?"

I didn't even know what she was talking about. "What's Scrum?" I thought.

Bob said, "No, we tried, but it didn't really work for us."

"For those of you not familiar with Scrum or Agile, I am a huge proponent. It's a methodology of running projects that has been proven to cut cost and time for delivering results. It centers around sprints that last about four weeks, and after four weeks, the team must deliver something useable. During the process, there is continuous testing, so end users will have ownership over what's delivered. The delivered product is not perfect, mind you. It's a minimal viable product, but it gets better with each sprint. For those of you unfamiliar with it, I strongly recommend the book *Scrum: The Art of Doing Twice the Work in Half the Time* by Jeff Sutherland[5]. If you don't have time to read, you can listen to it on your commute through Audible. You might want to make it required reading." We all wrote down the book title. I liked idea of faster delivery.

"When we do the detailed analysis of the top ideas that could produce the biggest impact, we want the idea we choose to deliver sustainable growth, not a quick one-time hit. The best idea will be selected as our project that we will MacGyver. We will estimate a return on investment for the project. This represents what the team thinks will be the financial return to the company. The result typically comes in the form of increased profits based on individuals receiving actionable information that helps them increase sales or seize new opportunities, but it could be from savings too.

"Remember, we will not necessarily follow best practices. We want fast, accurate results. We will implement best practices later when we have proven the idea is a winner. Then, we will create a team that will begin the process of preparing the data, which may mean a data mart, and designing how we will deliver the information. We may need new tools like a predictive tool, but we will do our best to work with what you have."

"In the process, your team will learn our *BAAM: Business Analytics Agile Methodology*. The beauty of *BAAM* is it's repeatable, so your team will use it for numerous projects in the future. When we deliver the project, we will have a retrospective and track the results. And of course, we will celebrate with each win," explained Ally.

Wow, Ally made it seem so easy. She broke it down into chunks. I loved the setting expectations aspect and thought that could really help us.

"Any questions?" Everyone shook their heads no.

"Great, we are almost done. What I want you to do now is grab a piece of paper, and for five minutes, you are going to write what would happen if you didn't move ahead with this and just did business as usual. What if your competition maximizes their use of data and analytics? Would you lose market share? How quickly? Jot down what you think the costs would be if you didn't change anything. Could you lose good IT people?"

"After you're done writing about the costs and risks of doing nothing, then write down how you define success on this project. What would it look like? How would you feel? How would your team feel? What would be the effect on the bottom line? Could you increase market share? Could you be seen as an innovative leader in your industry? There are no wrong answers. It doesn't even need to be in complete sentences; just write whatever comes to mind. I'll give you a warning halfway through to move to what it would mean for you to move forward and be hugely successful with BI. Ready, go!"

When the alarm finally went off, my hand hurt. I hadn't written that much in years. Massaging my hand, I said, "Ally, I would like to share my thoughts. I think we don't have a choice. I am super excited to do this and think we can conquer market share with your BI Bull's-eye approach. What about you, guys?" Everyone nodded.

"James, I think this has been the most productive meeting we've had in years, and I can't wait to go back to share this with my team! If you guys are committing to this, it's huge for us in IT. You will be giving us the support we have never had before. So, thank you!" Bob said as his eyes welled slightly.

"I think that's a fabulous point to end on and call it a day. It was long, but you played along with me, and for that, I honor you," Ally said as she put her hands together and slightly bowed.

"But, and I can say that word because I don't have any beads," Ally laughed, "I need to give the award for the beads to James, who stole all my beads and accumulated the most." Ally handed me a gift card. "You, my dear, get the active listener award." Ally reached over and started the music again. "We always end on a good note," she said with a huge smile.

I thanked Ally for an amazing day. I gave her a big hug before returning to my office. "Mind blowing!" I thought. We had hired consultants before, but nothing like this. Ally took topics we had been struggling with and led us through a process that got us to work as a team. We were comfortable making decisions rapidly because we knew it was okay to change our minds later if we were wrong. I love the idea of producing a minimal viable product. I had read somewhere that that was how Google tests innovations. If we could identify just a handful of key challenges that we could address with data and deliver timely information to make better decisions, like not extending credit to risky clients or having our salespeople pitch products that analytics tell us will be of interest to that specific client instead of whatever pops in their head, then we could significantly increase our profits.

I couldn't wait to get home to share my experience with Mary. Before I headed out, I decided it would be best if I rewrote my notes to make sure I didn't miss anything.

Key Takeaways:

- Establish and uphold meeting rules to maximize productivity.
- But is a blocking word. Use "yes and" to promote progress.
- Complete the Business Intelligence Action Assessment Indicator to identify current gaps. It's available at www.heatherized.com/bookbonus
- Use sticky notes for brainstorming creative ideas of the team.
- Time blocking by setting a timer in brainstorming exercises delivers rapid results.
- Before meetings measuring the state of the attendees helps increase communication and connection. Attendees simply give a score between 0-10 how they are feeling and a word.
- IT and business users often speak a different language.
- Business intelligence is not an IT thing, it should be an organizational initiative.
- Setting and reframing expectation when delivering business intelligence solutions increases end user satisfaction and adoption.

Heatherized

Hopefully you now understand the difference in funding a project and getting actively engaged in analytics. Congratulations you are significantly more advanced than you peers. But, you are not done yet. Greatness is a few pages away.

If you haven't downloaded the supplemental tools, please do so now. They are designed to help you maximize your business intelligence investment. Simply register at www.Heatherized.com/bookbonus, and you will gain access to many tools to aid you in your journey to become an analytic leader!

Here is what you'll receive:

- BI Action Assessment Indicator
- Core Values worksheet
- Questionnaires
- Sample job description for attracting BI superstars
- Videos to improve communication and provide time-saving methods
- And more!

Sign up today at www.Heatherized.com/BookBonus.

CHAPTER 5

Building Your Special Forces

"Talent wins games, but teamwork and intelligence wins championships."

–Michael Jordan

It was Wednesday. I woke early again and did my morning run to calm my brain and body. As I entered the kitchen, my wife handed me a cup of coffee and said, "Good morning, dear."

"Good morning, honey," I said, kissing her on the cheek, which seemed to startle her. "Hey, I may be a little late tonight. Ally is coming to the office today, and I have a lot I need to get done."

"Sure, thanks for telling me," she said with a slightly puzzled look on her face. "Babe, can I ask you a question?"

"Of course."

"Is there something else going on? Should I be concerned? You are getting up earlier, you float around the house, and heck, you just kissed me on the cheek."

I laughed, "Why, can't you tell? I am in love, my dear," I chuckled. Her face went pale. "No, hon, you are the love of my life," I said, patting her bottom. "But I am in love with my work again. I am so energized and hopeful that we can accomplish something great."

"Sounds like Ally has a spell on you, but as long as you are happy and faithful, I like it," she said, whacking me hard on the butt.

I can't believe it's only been five days since Ally changed our world. Even Mary had noticed it. Ally was like a lightning bolt of energy, getting everyone on the executive team excited. It wasn't just me; I had observed that everyone was coming into the office a little earlier. They were smiling and laughing more. What was odd about it was that it had a trickle-down effect to the whole organization. I was not sure what was happening. It was like they had hope again. They knew positive change was coming.

After the last meeting, Ally asked us to digest what we had learned and to start communicating with our teams that our BI initiative was under new management. I had been working hard on setting expectations and reframing them and had asked my team to do so as well. We had all read the Scrum book and loved the concept, but I had my concerns that the older team members wouldn't embrace this transformation. A few had expressed that things weren't broken. They questioned why we needed to change everything.

That day, we were scheduled to have a brief review meeting with Ally and then discuss the team and what skills the team should have. I really didn't understand the point of this meeting because we already had our BI team in place, but Ally's energy was like a drug, and she hadn't steered us wrong yet.

Sarah handed me my second cup of coffee. I made sure to tell Sarah that I appreciated it instead of taking it for granted, and I headed into my office. Sarah walked in with a small stack of papers and said, "Ally asked me to print out 20 copies of our most recent job postings for a Business Intelligence Manager/Analyst. The weird thing was that she asked me to print them on colored paper. Do you mind taking those with you? Ally is already in the Chicago room if you want to chat with her," Sarah said with a flirtatious look that implied I had a crush on Ally.

"Oh, thanks. I wonder what she's going to do with these." I checked my email, grabbed the stack of job postings and my coffee, and headed to the Chicago room where I could already hear Ally's music playing.

"Good morning, Ally! Sarah asked me to give you these."

"Fabulous, she found colored paper!" I gave her an inquisitive look, to which she responded, "James, you know I am not going to share the secret until it's time," and batted her eyelashes.

"I suppose," I said as the others entered the room.

Ally looked at her watch. "Wow, you are all early. Love it. Are you guys cool if we start early?"

"Yes, let's get started. I think we are all anxious to see what you have in store for us today," I said. Everyone nodded.

"Before we start, let's each give our number, and today, I want to know what you think was the most impactful thing you learned in our last meeting. If someone before you has stated the same concept you learned, just acknowledge it and share another item. When you are done, you will call on someone else to share. Bob, we will start with you."

"I am an eight, and I learned that you guys are willing to do what it takes to actively engage in this initiative, and my team is very excited. Mark?"

"8.5. I realized we were caught in the spin cycle and expecting IT to magically deliver. I love the sticky note exercise and started using it with my team. Susan?"

"Nine. I love all your teaching techniques and have already set up a training initiative for the entire organization that will start with setting expectations. I think this can increase productivity as well as employee and customer satisfaction. Chris?"

"Eight. I learned that I am a big part of the problem. My team reminded me that I don't even use the dashboard that IT designed for me, and I didn't communicate why it doesn't work for me. I dump data into Excel," Chris said with an embarrassed look on his face. "But I am 100% committed to working with IT and being a better role model. James?"

"Nine. I agree with Susan on expectations. That was huge. But if I had to choose something else, I think the bull's-eye exercise was impactful. I want to personally apologize to Bob and his team for not being a better..." I looked at Ally and smiled, "...a better analytic leader." Ally and everyone clapped.

"Fabulous. You guys are doing awesome. Today is a big day because we get to be artists, and we are also going to define the skills and attributes we want to develop in our team members. Remember when we talked about people, processes, tools, and data, and I said that people are the secret sauce? And yes, we will need sticky notes. But before we talk about the people, I want to do a little exercise."

Ally handed out two blank white pieces of paper to each person along with a small box of colored pencils. Ally giggled, "It's time to get creative! I know you guys aren't artists, but what we want to do is wake up the right side, the creative side, of your brains. Neuroscience has proven that we can build new neural pathways late into life. One way to work on the right side is by adding color and by drawing. So, each of you is going to draw what you used to think about business intelligence on one sheet, and on the other sheet, you will draw what your vision for BI is in your organization. There are no wrong answers, but you must draw pictures. For example, Chris, if you used to think BI was a money pit, you would draw a money pit," Ally said as she set the timer for 15 minutes.

I felt a little awkward using colored pencils and drawing. Ally was pushing me way out of my comfort zone, but I agreed to be all in. I started drawing stick people with black horn-rimmed glasses to symbolize IT with a couple dashboards. Then, I drew another person who looked frustrated to represent myself.

Ally walked around, looking at the pictures and smiling. I laughed as I started the second drawing. For my vision of BI, I sketched "data" in the cloud, a circle of people holding hands, dashboards that rained money, and three ships in an arrow formation. The front boat was significantly ahead of the others and had a Playfair Distributing flag. I smiled as I admired my work.

Ally had each of us present our artwork, and we had a good laugh. What was amazing was that, for the most part, we had the same vision of what BI success looked like.

"Congratulations," she said, clapping her hands. "It appears you all have a similar concept of success! I would like you to take a moment to reflect on the difference in what you used to think about BI and your future vision."

I laughed out loud. The difference was significant. "We've come a long way," I said.

"Yes, you have!" Ally said, flashing her vibrant smile. "Now, we are going to explore what team members you need to utilize to deliver on your vision."

"We have a BI team," Bob said. "And they are very excited to get going."

"That's fabulous, Bob, but part of the process is to make sure we are putting the right butts in the right seats. It's not recommended to just put a body in a position. Where is the BI initiative in the list of strategic priorities for the organization?"

"It's at the top!" I blurted.

"Well, if you were in the military, and you had a mission that was the most important mission planned, who would you put on it?"

"The Navy SEALs or one of the special forces teams," Chris said.

"Exactly! But I must ask, have you been allocating your top talent to your BI initiative in the past?"

"No," Mark said with a guilty look on his face. "I have to admit, when Bob asked for someone from my department to work with his team, I gave them an intern because I figured I wouldn't miss them. I'm sorry, Bob. I guess I just was ignorant."

Bob sat up in his chair with pride. "It's okay, Mark, that's the past. I think we all have a better understanding of what we need to do. Ally, how do we know which butts to put in the seats?"

"How do you think we will determine that?" Ally asked, running her fingers through her hair and flashing her sassy smile as she handed each of us a stack of sticky notes.

"Let me guess. A timed brainstorming session with sticky notes, maybe?" said Bob.

"Wow, you are catching on," she said, touching Bob's shoulder. "What you will do is write down what attributes or skills you think people on the team should have. Now, you may write something down that you only need one or two people to have, like SQL skills, but let's get some attributes documented. I want to challenge you to not just include knowledge or skill-based items but include some core values. For example, in our organization, we won't bring someone on if they are not a lifelong learner. We only want people with inquisitive minds because we believe people who are inquisitive love a challenge and do what it takes to solve complex problems. Does that make sense?"

"Yes. I guess I never looked at it that way, but that completely makes sense. Discovering if someone is a lifelong learner would be pretty easy in an interview too. We would just need to ask them what they read last or what they are currently learning. I like it," said Susan.

"Okay, you have 15 minutes. There are no wrong answers, and you will write what skills your special forces need for BI success. Don't just focus on the people you like the most. Some of you may be tempted to think about the people currently on your teams, and I encourage you not to do that! We want to look at this from a clean slate. Later, we will look at team members, where they fit, and if we need to give some of them extra training. Ready, set, go."

My mind was racing. Ideas were flooding in as I scribbled on each sticky note. Perseverance, a positive attitude, predictive expertise, industry knowledge, teamwork, BI knowledge, communication skills, active listening...

"Seven minutes," Ally said. Wow, that went fast. More ideas filled my head. Before I knew it, the alarm went off.

"Okay," Ally said. "Let's start with some core values we want the team to have, and then, we will look at more specific knowledge or skills of individual team members. Finally, we will place your team members into the seats. We may have gaps. This might mean you need to hire someone, bring in a consultant, or send your team members to training."

I hadn't noticed it at the time, but Ally had a stack of sticky notes too. On the top of a flip chart, she wrote "core values."

"Who would like to start to share the core values they came up with? Core values are non-negotiable attributes or qualities the people must possess as a team member. As we go through them, eliminate any duplicates you have, and if you come up with a new one, just jot it down."

One by one, we shared our core values, Ally sharing her ideas last. We then prioritized the list and agreed on what Ally called the "non-negotiables." Ally explained that many organizations make the mistake of looking for a specific skill instead of core values. She said that when team members don't all have the core values, it eventually creates friction and toxicity in the organization.

This really made me think. Maybe we needed to examine the core values of all our employees. Ally had us pick the top five to seven core values that we decided were non-negotiable, and we all agreed on a basic definition of why each was necessary. In the end, we agreed on the core values of:

1. Integrity & candor – Builds trust while calling out landmines

2. Service to others – Understanding they are serving and leaving their egos at the door

3. Accountable – Admits to errors or lack of knowledge so team can work together to resolve challenges

4. Perseverance & resourcefulness – A can-do attitude and will do what it takes to accomplish task

5. Growth mindset – Lifelong learner with an inquisitive mind

6. Passionate team player – We want people who care and will support each other. No knowledge hoarding or acting superior allowed.

As we went through the process, I realized that we did have some people that didn't fit our core values on our team. It was a sinking feeling. My face must have conveyed what I was feeling because Ally said, "James, you have an interesting look on your face. Maybe you would like to share what you are feeling or thinking?"

"Ahh, sure," I said uneasily. "Well, first, I think maybe we need to do this exercise for the entire organization. I think these same values would probably apply."

I glanced at Susan, who was nodding her head yes.

"Second, I realized that we may have people in our organization that don't have these core values. I can't speak for the rest of you, but I think most of the people we have had to let go in the past often lacked one of these core values."

Ally said, "Great insight. It's not uncommon for clients to have this experience. It's natural. Think about someone that you had to let go in the past. How much time was spent trying to make them successful? Imagine if, for your BI team and your company, you only hired people with these key attributes? Do you think your teams would be more productive?"

"Ha," Bob laughed. "We had a guy named Grant, and we were always trying to get him in line. He was brilliant, but when things went south, it was never his fault. We tried to explain that if he just told us something was wrong, we could fix it together. But he never gave anyone a heads up when things were going to blow up. Then, when something blew up or a delivery date was missed, it was never his fault. No accountability, but he was brilliant. The team hated working with Grant."

Next, Ally had us share the skills we thought we needed on the team. "These are typically more role-specific. Don't worry about the individuals just yet. We want to define what skills or knowledge we need, and then, we will cluster them into the seats. Finally, we will examine your team and determine which butts fit in each seat. Don't forget that this is just for your special forces BI and analytics team. When we define the seats first and we communicate the seats with an agile approach, the team will start to self-form. Think about it. You all know who has what talents, and so do your team members. When they know the mission and know each other's talent, if given the option, they could probably create the best team. It's like in gym class when you were a kid. The jocks would try to get on the same team so they could kill the nerds," Ally laughed.

"When we define the seats, we frequently end up with a situation where some of the current BI team members don't have the skills we need for a specific project. However, if they are talented, we want to keep them and have them serve as report writers. Our goal then will be to create a plan for them to build the missing skills or knowledge." Ally looked at Susan. I glanced at Bob, who looked relieved that there was going to be a place for everyone on his team.

"Bob, does that make sense to you?" Ally asked.

"Yes, thank you. I was already thinking that a couple of my team members were good but not special forces good."

"That's absolutely normal. It's been my experience that if they understand why we are changing the approach and they understand why they aren't on the special forces team yet, then they work are to get on it. If they don't work hard, they are typically missing a core value and, eventually, they may leave the company. Having people leave is not bad. If they don't fit the culture, they will be happier somewhere else."

Ally had us go through each of our skill lists and put them on the flip chart labeled "specific skills of the team":

Aptitude for BI and predictive tools
Scrum experience
Emotional intelligence
Good communicator (verbal, non-verbal, written)
Positive attitude
Doesn't fear failure
Knows our business
Knowledge of functional area

SQL skills

ETL skills

Data expertise

Statistics, mathematics, or analytic background

Knowledge of Cognos (our BI tool)

Active listener

Influential/respected

Likeable

Good storyteller

As we went through our sticky notes, briefly discussing each skill, Mark said, "I am a little confused. Doesn't it depend on what problem we are looking to solve? For example, if it's a problem with returns and we want to predict inventory better, we would need a different team than the one we would need for an issue with the marketing message and predicting sales."

Ally's green eyes beamed, and she leaped toward Mark, "Exactly!!!"

Mark excitedly said, "Oh, I get it! That's why we use Scrum. Yes, I read the Scrum book," he bragged. "The teams self-form based on the project. I am sorry. My mind still thinks in the old way where the BI team is a fixed team from IT."

Wow, I hadn't made that connection either. It was like a puzzle piece fit perfectly. The teams are agile and dynamic. This is brilliant. You could feel the energy in the room heighten. Ally bounced back to the front of the room and said, "Let's have a little fun!" She pulled out the stack of colored paper that had the most recent job posting for a business analyst.

"I want to read you the most recent job posting you guys used to recruit top talent. So, as I read this, I want you to put yourself in the mindset and emotion of the superstar you want on your team. Would you respond to this post, and is this post what you really want on your team?"

Experience and Other Requirements:

- One to three years of experience with advanced level of business analysis with emphasis on business intelligence, ETL development, data warehousing, and advanced analytics projects

- Experience with the full Microsoft Stack (SSRS, SSIS, SSAS) and relational database design, development & documentation experience required

- Demonstrates strong problem-solving skills

- Experience writing SQL, transactional SQL (stored procedures, triggers, and functions), and extensive experience with index tuning strategies and complex query optimization in MS SQL Server required

- Detailed knowledge of Cognos Express including Framework Manager

- Strong understanding of cross browsers and cross platform compatibility issues and solutions

- Excellent oral and written communication skills

- Demonstrates conceptual thinking and analytical skills

- Demonstrates teamwork in all interactions with coworkers and in the completion of all duties and responsibilities

- Must be capable of working multiple projects at one time and evaluate/prioritize as necessary

- Working knowledge of PCs, MS Windows application software packages, Microsoft network, and financial institution experience helpful.

Interpersonal Skills

- Courtesy, tact, and diplomacy are essential elements of the job.

I started laughing, and so did Bob and the others. "Why are you laughing? Ally asked with her sassy smile.

"It's fabulous if we are looking for nerdy IT people and focusing on skills, but it's been my experience that highly analytical people with these skills are not usually the best when it comes to interpersonal skills. I really like the 'courtesy, tact, and diplomacy,'" I chuckled.

"If you are a superstar, would you respond to this job posting?" Ally asked.

"No. I would not see the challenge in this job. I would be asking what's in it for me! What's my opportunity? We don't even talk about that," said Chris.

"Oh my gosh, you are right!" Susan exclaimed. "We know a good business analyst is really hard to find, but we aren't selling the opportunity. We are filtering on skills."

"I give you credit," Ally said, putting her hand on Susan's shoulder. "At least you mention the interpersonal skills. Most don't. But Chris is right. It doesn't mention that they will get advanced training or challenging and interesting work that impacts the entire organization. You need to make it appealing to the superstars that are in high demand. So, what would you do differently?"

"Maybe I could work with the marketing team to create a job post that would sell the position to the superstar we are looking for," Susan said, looking at Mark.

"Wow, that's a fabulous idea because, Mark, I bet you have someone good at creating compelling copy, right?"

Mark nodded. "Absolutely, we would love to help. And I think we need to emphasize the core values. Bob, correct me if I am wrong, but if they are inquisitive and somewhat smart, they could learn the tools. We have been focusing on the tools and not someone skilled in collaboration."

"You're right! We've been doing this all wrong. As Ally said earlier, people are the secret sauce, and we have been looking for the wrong people. I'll be the first to admit, IT people, myself included, aren't usually the most social people. We tend to be introverted. Ally, is it realistic to find superstars?" asked Bob.

"Great observation, Bob. And it is hard to find superstars, or unicorns, as I sometimes call them, but there are some out there. However, it's possible to train the right people who want to learn— you know, the growth-minded people. I am living proof! By nature, I am introverted." Everyone laughed.

"No, really. What you don't know is, as much as I love working with clients like you, it's exhausting to me. I am an IT/finance geek and thought my career would allow me to hide behind a computer crunching numbers. But I realized I had to learn to communicate with the business. So, yes, the right people can be trained. Are we in agreement that your old job post sucks?"

"Yes!" we all shouted.

"Okay, then we need to celebrate that! We all agree that we are looking for champions, right?" Ally asked as she handed each of us a few sheets of the colored job postings.

"So, shred these old job posts into confetti, and when I play the music, toss it," Ally laughed. She hit play on her phone. The beats of the *Rocky* theme song filled the room. I felt like Rocky on the steps, throwing my hands in the air but with confetti. The entire team was smiling, and Ally was dancing in the front of the room. When the song ended, she jokingly asked, "What's your number?" There was no doubt we were all at 10.

After a short break, Ally said, "Now, I am going to give you another secret that was game-changing for me when I started using it. It's the simplest technique, and I want you to start using it regularly. Are you ready?" Ally raised her eyebrow. "This question should be asked with every project you have and should be asked regularly because the answers change. The questions is:

"What's your greatest fear or concern with this project?"

"Have you ever asked that question to your teams? When you ask it, you receive insight from everyone's perspectives and discover what people fear. Once you know what people fear, you can address it. Most of the time, fear is based on uncertainty. It comes from not knowing what will happen or how something will be handled. When you eliminate fear and uncertainty, you foster collaboration!"

We sat there, stunned. It was a simple question, but I know I had never asked it.

"Bob, what do people typically fear when implementing new software?" Ally asked, turning to Bob.

"Well, my team fears failure, and the users typically fear new technology, looking stupid, or they sometimes fear that the technology will eliminate their jobs. It doesn't help that every day in the paper, there is another article about artificial intelligence replacing millions of jobs. Hmm, and we wonder why end users aren't excited when we say we are exploring how to use AI."

"Exactly," Ally said. "So, let's try this now. What are you afraid of or concerned about regarding your new BI and analytics project? Bob, we will start with you."

"Finding the talent. The 'unicorns' as you called them."

"Great. Team, what can we do to help ease this concern for Bob?"

Mary jumped in: "I think we already stated it. I will work with marketing, and we are going to modify our job posting for the open position we have right now."

"Fabulous. Mark, what is your fear?"

"If I give you my top talent as a subject matter expert, I am worried that I will be short-handed and might miss our targets," said Mark.

"Mark, maybe we could revisit your team's quarterly objectives to adjust them so we can make this a priority," I said.

"Fabulous," said Mark. "That could give us some breathing room."

We continued though the entire team, creating ideas to address everyone's top concerns. It felt as if a pressure value had been released on all of us. It was liberating. I imagined how much less stressed the entire organization would feel if everyone asked that one question.

Team members would feel like their voices mattered. Everyone would collaborate to help resolve the issue. I could image that someone's concern could bring to light a potential major landmine that no one else realized existed. I was in awe that it was so simple. One question!

As Ally wrapped up the day, she had each of us share two things we learned. She then challenged us to identify the players we thought might qualify for our special forces team. These were to be people we might need in the future depending on the subject area we were tackling. Ally explained this would be a larger group, and from that, we would select a smaller group for each initiative.

"When you choose your team members to invite, we only want those that you believe possess the cores values we defined. Remember, core values are non-negotiable. If you have a team member in mind but they don't have all the skills or knowledge we identified, that is okay. We will create mentoring and training opportunities for them. Our goal is to grow your team to be special forces to reduce the cost of expensive consultants. When people learn that they have been selected to be part of a special forces team, they really step up. I have also found that rock stars are inspired and motivated to work with other top talent. It's fun to watch how people respond. They all level up!"

"Now, you may be wondering what will happen to those who don't have the core values and aren't invited." Heads were nodding.

"Candidly, some may leave! But that's okay. I've found that when people are not a good fit culturally and don't share the core values, they typically aren't happy anyway. There may be some that you think are on the fence. I recommend that you invite those individuals to the next meeting but explain that the team will be reduced and that you aren't sure if they have what it takes. Tell them the core values that are required, and challenge them to show they have those core values. Express that you believe they have them, but you owe it to the whole team to only invite the superstars. Some of the people on the fence will step up, and others will call a recruiter."

"I strongly recommend communicating that this is the direction of the company from the top down. Tell them that the people who step up and make the special forces team will be rewarded with interesting projects, respect, training, and compensation. There will be some people that don't step up but have the core values. Those people could still serve your organization well, but set expectations that they will be limited in their growth. There are usually one or two people you absolutely know do not have the cores values. You are probably thinking of someone right now."

I swear, Ally can read my mind at times.

"Susan, please chime in on this, but I recommend that you have a frank discussion with those team members. Tell them what will be expected of them, and state that you realize they may not be on board. They may not be willing or able to make the transition, and that's okay. Tell them to think about it for a few days and let them decide. If they decide they are not a good fit, tell them the organization will help them find a job somewhere else and give them a letter of recommendation."

Bob blurred out, "What if they say they are in just to keep their jobs and don't make the changes necessary?"

"Great question. Typically, they find the new environment so uncomfortable that they will leave on their own, or their performance will not meet the new expectations and you will have to work with Susan on the process to terminate them. We only want rock stars! It's kind of like basketball. Why did LeBron James decide to leave Cleveland, a town that loved him, in 2010? If you recall, he left and went to the Miami Heat."

Mark emphatically said, "He wanted to win a championship!"

"Yes! Superstars want to play with superstars! So, can you guys commit to inviting only people with core values that can contribute to the skills and knowledge we need for our special forces? To be an analytic leader, you have to make the tough decisions sometimes."

"I'm in," I said. The others all followed.

At the end of the meeting, I returned to my office to copy my notes and document my thoughts. I found that my meeting review session really helped to solidify what I was learning.

Key Takeaways:

- Drawing colored pictures of vision and ideas helps communication and creativity.
- Allocate top talent to your business intelligence initiatives.
- Define the seats or roles first then put the right people in the right seats instead of putting warm bodies in the seats.
- Define core values that all team members must possess.
- Hire for core values and ability to learn instead of technology skills.
- Job postings should be written to attract top talent by sharing what is in t it for the candidate.
- Celebrate accomplishments and small victories.

Key questions to ask on all projects is: What's your greatest fear or concern with this project?

Heatherized

If you have taken the time to read this far, you must believe that data and analytics is important to your organization's future. But, are you putting your best people on the team? Don't worry if you have been hiring the wrong skills, you should now have a better idea of what you should look for to develop internal talent. In the supplemental tools there is a sample job description, for you to share with your human resources team.

If you haven't accessed the supplemental tools, please do so now. They are designed to help you maximize your business intelligence investment. Simply register at www.Heatherized.com/bookbonus, and you will gain access to many tools to aid you in your journey to become an analytic leader!

Here is what you'll receive:

- BI Action Assessment Indicator
- Core Values worksheet
- Questionnaires
- Sample job description for attracting BI superstars
- Videos to improve communication and provide time-saving methods
- And more!

Sign up today at www.Heatherized.com/BookBonus.

CHAPTER 6

All In

*"It is not the strongest of the species that survives,
nor the most intelligent that survives. It is the
one that is most adaptable to change."*

–Charles Darwin

It was a bright, crisp morning during my run along the water. It was unusual to see dolphins in the bay this early, but as I ran, there was a beautiful dolphin swimming in the same direction. It was as if he was running with me, cheering me on. "Everyone needs cheerleaders in life," I thought. But even more importantly, I thought, "We need good advisors and coaches."

I was at the point in my life where I guess I thought I knew everything I needed to know. I was comfortable in my lifestyle, but looking back, I felt stale and bored. Since meeting Ally and having her challenge me and the team, I felt alive again. I was so grateful for being open to seeing things differently. If I hadn't sat next to Ally on the plane, life would be very different. If she had called into my organization and pitched her services, I am pretty sure I would have said that we already had BI consultants. It's funny how the universe sometimes sets up situations and introduces you to people when you need them most.

Today was the big meeting with the larger team. The executives had met earlier and personally reviewed each candidate for the team. Ally had provided tools to help evaluate team members and whether they possessed the required core values. Each candidate was personally invited by an executive who explained the expectations. It was fun to watch the candidates sit taller when they realized they were invited to this special, exclusive event. The executive team was asked to help lead the initial sessions to communicate the plan as well as why and how it would work. I was to do the initial introduction, and then Bob would share ideas on how the BI initiative was under new management.

As I entered the large conference room, there was a buzz. The energy and excitement engulfed me. Everyone had taken their seats and had journals open to take notes. The meeting wasn't even supposed to start for five minutes. Clearly, our new practice of starting right on time was working. I smiled.

"Welcome, James," Ally said, bouncing over to give me a hug. "Are you ready for the big day?" she whispered in my ear.

"Absolutely," I responded. We had worked for a week on the meeting outline, with Ally's guidance, of course. This was transformation day. We started by explaining why we needed to change and what we learned over the last few weeks of working with Ally. We admitted that we had failed our team and that we discovered we were not good analytic leaders. We committed to changing. I discussed the expectations, why each person in the room was invited, and that they had to be personally nominated by someone on the executive team. I looked around the room. Attendees were sitting up in their seats, leaning slightly forward, and engaged with big, prideful smiles.

Bob then shared how the IT team was working on transforming too but that they needed everyone's help.

"Changes don't happen overnight, and IT, just like everyone in this room, is going to be challenged to learn new things, step out of their comfort zone, and level up. We will fail at times. But failure is to be embraced as a learning experience. Our goal is that if we are going to fail, we will fail fast and learn. Everyone will need to communicate, share ideas, and not be afraid to be creative. We will need to all be supportive of each other and collaborate. Today, Ally is going to teach you a lot of things that she has already taught the executive team. In the few weeks that we have worked with Ally, we have found that her 'little secrets,'" he said, making air quotes, "have been life-changing. If you listen and commit to being all in, I am certain you will have a similar experience." The entire executive team nodded. "Ally, I am going to hand it over to you." Applause filled the room.

Ally beamed. "Thank you, but you guys are the heroes. You are doing all the work, not me. I am just your guide on this journey."

"Today, I am going to address the first challenge we will have, and that's finding time. Does anyone have too much time?" The room chuckled, and Ally proceeded to introduce them to time blocking, expectations, and reframing and introduced them to Scrum.

In the afternoon, the executives reviewed the strategic goals. Then, Ally walked them through the components of business intelligence and analytics, having them draw pictures. I felt better knowing they were as bad as we were at drawing. Ally took the opportunity to show everyone my drawing, which resulted in a lot of laughter. Throughout the day, she had them play games and do exercises to keep them engaged. It was amazing to watch everyone embrace the concepts. At the end of the day, Ally challenged the group.

"Did you learn something today that could improve your life?" she asked.

Everyone responded, "Yes!" I had never seen this group so attentive.

"Your job is to share the life-changing parts with other people you know. But some of you might be feeling a little overwhelmed. And that's okay. This is overwhelming, and honestly, it's not for everyone. Or maybe it's right for you, but it is just not the right time in your life to commit to this dramatic change. Tomorrow, we will have another exciting day, but if you decide tonight that this is not for you, please just talk to your manager. You will not be eliminated from participation in this team in the future. Some of you may have a lot of family stuff going on. You might be dealing with a sick parent or child. Personally, I think it shows more character if you only commit to things that you can give 100 percent. Just know it's okay to opt out. This is the special forces, and if you can't give 100 percent, you will be hurting the rest of the team and yourself. So, please only show up in this room tomorrow if you are 100 percent in."

"If you are in, when you get home tonight, think about what you learned today. I recommend reviewing your notes tonight, and tomorrow, we will introduce you to the MacGyver approach, which is a cornerstone of the *Business Intelligence Bull's-eye Framework*. One of the exercises we will be doing tomorrow that you can get a head start on is to brainstorm creative ways that Fairplay Distributing can leverage data and predictive analytics to increase efficiency. Pretend you have a crystal ball that provides insight into your business. What would you ask to see?"

"And with that challenge, I want to thank each and every one of you for an amazing day! You guys worked hard and played all out. Well done!" Ally clapped her hands, and everyone joined in.

I sat back and watched the people. They didn't want to leave. They stood up but stayed. The room was buzzing. I overheard one of the IT guys say, "I am feeling exhausted. For an introvert like me, this is a lot. But at the same time, I don't want to miss anything."

One of the marketing girls laughed and said to Steve, "Thank you for the opportunity. I feel like I am finally one of the cool kids in high school."

The room finally dissipated, and I walked to the front where Ally was packing up. "How did they do?" I asked.

"I think you are going to have a great team. The challenge will be to not let old practices slip back in. But you guys are definitely on the right path. What did you think?" inquired Ally, raising her right eyebrow.

"I have never had so much fun in an all-day meeting. I know you said we could leave, but I wanted to stay and show my support and how much this means to the organization. I noticed a couple people were a little hesitant at first, but then, they seemed to connect. I think this was amazing. Can't wait until tomorrow."

Key Takeaways:

- Personally invite only people possessing the core values to be part of the business intelligence team..
- If team members can't give 100 percent, they will be hurting the team and themselves.
- It's okay for team member to not want to be on the special forces team.

You are making it happen. Learning to be an analytic leader takes time and work, but you are in the elite group of executives committed to excellence! Congratulations on your commitment to becoming an analytic leader. To maximize the value of reading this book, you should access the supplemental materials. Simply register at www. Heatherized.com/bookbonus, and you will gain access to many tools to aid you in your journey to become an analytic leader!

Here is what you'll receive:

- BI Action Assessment Indicator
- Core Values worksheet
- Questionnaires
- Sample job description for attracting BI superstars
- Videos to improve communication and provide time-saving methods
- And more!

Sign up today at www.Heatherized.com/BookBonus.

CHAPTER 7

Crazy Ideas Welcome!

"Don't measure yourself by what you have accomplished, but by what you should have accomplished with your ability."

–John Wooden

Dawn came early. I didn't realize how exhausting transformational change could be. As I walked downstairs, the smell of coffee and pancakes overcame me.

"Good morning, honey. I decided you needed victory pancakes this morning," Mary said as I entered the kitchen. I smiled, recalling all the Saturday mornings that Mary make victory pancakes for the kids before their soccer games when they were younger. She poured the batter into the shape of a V, which made it challenging to flip, but Mary had it mastered.

"Yes, it is a big day! Man, I crashed last night. I don't even remember my head hitting the pillow," I laughed.

"Well, that's because you fell asleep before it hit," Mary said, handing me a warm plate with a perfectly formed V pancake.

"Thanks, dear. The pancakes mean a lot. I was going to go for a run this morning, but I think I'll head in early today. It will be interesting to see if anyone opts out of the program. Today, we start to define the one project our special forces team will focus on. I have so many ideas, but I'm even more anxious to see what they come up with."

"I don't know what you are paying this Ally girl, but if the rest of your team is as excited and energized as you are, it's not enough. I feel like I should cook her dinner," Mary laughed.

"You just want to meet her," I said, finishing up the large pancake and kissing Mary on the cheek. "Maybe, when this is all done, we will take her and her husband out to dinner."

I arrived at the office and entered the kitchen relieved to see someone had already started the coffee. Sarah hadn't arrived yet, so I poured a cup. "Good morning, James," Susan said as she walked in to grab a Diet Coke out of the refrigerator. "Curious, what did you think of yesterday?"

"I thought it was amazing. I am so proud of everyone, and the energy level was outstanding," I said.

"I agree," said Susan, turning toward me. "You know, I received a number of emails yesterday after the event, and people are very excited. A couple of them mentioned they are happy to see that the executives are willing to listen to their ideas. This is a great change. In the past, we have seen comments in exit interviews that people felt that they didn't really matter and that no one listened to them. I think our new challenge will be keeping the momentum."

"You are right. Maybe we should talk to Ally about that," I said, wiping up the cream I spilled on the counter. "I would love to chat, but I need to brainstorm a little before we meet. Whatever we decide to MacGyver today could make a big impact on the bottom line."

"I understand," Susan said, grabbing a napkin and following me out of the kitchen.

At 8:45, I walked to the conference room where Ally's music was already playing. I thought I was early, only to find half the room full. People were talking in small groups and jotting down ideas. Interestingly, the groups were not divided by departments. In fact, each of the clusters had a mix of people from various departments. In past meetings, everyone sat in groups by departments, and it resulted in an us-versus-them environment. Sally from marketing was among a group of three people near the window. She asked, "Mr. Brown, would you like to join us? We are brainstorming ideas for AI."

"I would love to. Thanks. I wish I had known you guys were all here early. I was in my office brainstorming alone," I said, pulling up a chair and opening my notebook. I thought to myself, "This is amazing. Everyone is so into this."

Josh from IT was tapping away on his computer. "Look, I found an article on Amazon's automation of their warehouses with robots." I closely examined people's faces in the different groups. They had an excitement in their eyes, almost a look of wonder and awe. They started scribbling notes and discussing which distribution center would be best to test out robots. I just smiled and continued to observe the room.

At 9 a.m. sharp, everyone was already in their seats working when Ally turned off the music and said, "Welcome back to day two!" She scanned the room.

"It looks like we have a couple people who have decided they can't commit to giving 100 percent at this time, and I want to make sure everyone knows that's okay. I applaud their honesty with themselves and with the team. But I also want to make sure every one of you makes them feel welcome to continue to share their ideas. In fact, just because you're part of a special team doesn't mean you are better than others. It means you were chosen to be a leader in the organization's transformation. But as a transformational leader, it's even more important that you make everyone feel like they are part of it. Ask their opinions, and get their ideas. Can you do that?" Everyone nodded. "Great, then let's rock and roll."

"Today, our goal is to brainstorm and create a mountain of ideas on how data and analytics can help us achieve our strategic goals. We discussed the strategic goals yesterday, and I have listed them on this flip chart as a reference point. In brainstorming, we will set a timer, and we celebrate what?"

"Crazy ideas," everyone responded.

"Exactly. When we brainstorm, there are no limits. We never use the word '*but.*' Instead, we say what?"

"Yes and," Everyone chanted. It was amazing how she had trained them in one day.

"What we will do is brainstorm for 20 minutes. I know many of you started this already, and that's extraordinary. Just keep building on your lists. Then, we will get in groups and share our ideas. Groups must have at least one person from each department. As you review the ideas, you may create new ideas. Then, each team will create a list of their ideas on a flip chart and individually vote on the ideas they feel are the best. When you vote, you need to consider the impact on the bottom line and the feasibility of delivering it in 90 days. You might want to consider if the data is collected currently and where it's stored."

"To vote, you will each get three colored circles. The green is your very top selection, the yellow is your middle, and the red will go on your third choice. Once everyone votes, your group will agree on which three ideas they will present to the larger group. Once all the groups have presented their top three ideas, we will discuss and prioritize them. Our goal is to narrow the list to the ultimate top three. When we have the ultimate top three ideas, we will run a deeper analysis and estimate the forecasted ROI of each initiative. Any questions?"

"Will each section be timed?" Steve asked.

"Absolutely. That's part of the magic. If we didn't time it, we could be here for years," Ally laughed. "I will tell you how much time you have for each section and give you a halfway and two-minute warning. James, did you want to say anything before we get started?"

"Yes, if you don't mind. The way I look at our business, there are three main areas that are of the utmost concern: financial management, inventory management, and customer management. For example, if we are slow in the accounts receivable process, we could have a cash flow problem that could reduce a company's ability to invest in new inventory. That, in turn, can negatively impact customer service. Ally, I had noted some Key Performance Indicators, also called KPIs, that we discussed. Maybe we should do a refresher on those before we start. I believe the teams can use these ideas and make them bigger and better. Let's do a little 'yes and' exercise."

"Great idea, James." Ally handed me a green marker as I approached the flip chart at the front of the room. At the top, I wrote "Financial Management" followed by the KPIs,[6] which I explained briefly.

Financial Management

- Collection time for accounts receivables
- Sales and revenue performance
- Gross margin performance
- Days sales outstanding
- Working capital availability
- Accounts payable turnover
- Inventory turnover

Flipping the page, I grabbed the red market and wrote "Inventory Management." "Guys, this is our biggest expense. Our goal is to keep it lean but not run out of product. This could be where predictive analytics could really help us out, but I want your thoughts." I then listed the KPIs and briefly described each. I was careful to avoid acronyms and assumed that not everyone knew the terms. That seemed to put everyone at ease.

Inventory Management

- Inventory holding costs
- Inventory turnover rates
- Average inventory
- Average days to sell inventory
- Obsolete inventory carrying costs/write-off costs
- Order fulfillment rates
- Number of backorders

"And finally, we have customer management. This includes everything we need to know about making our customers happy and selling them what they will buy. I think predictive analytics in this area could help us gain market share, and based on last quarter, our competitors in some regions may be starting to do this. Have you ever noticed how it's as if Amazon knows what you want before you do? And they even know what color you would want," I laughed.

"Well, they are using advanced analytics to decide what to show you and what deals they offer you. So, here are some of the KPIs we defined, but I know you guys will take this to a whole new level and add ideas for predictive analytics." Flipping the page, I wrote down:

Customer Management

- Customer order volume and frequency
- Average shipping times
- Delivery efficiency
- Customer backorders
- Time needed to fulfill backorders
- Margin breakdown for individual customers, products, product lines, etc.

"Does this help?" I asked, observing a room of nodding heads. "Great. Now you will take these concepts and expand them. Any more questions about the process for Ally?"

Ally moved to the front of the room. "Thanks, James. Those KPIs give us a good view of data points that can help, but I want to make sure you guys take this a bit further. I want you to get creative. Let's say one of the KPIs is trending in the wrong direction. What question will you ask next?"

"Why?" said someone in the back of the room.

"Exactly, you keep asking why. So, as you explore ideas, keep asking why. But then flip it. Ask yourself, 'If I could have insights my competitors don't, what would I want to know?'"

"Let me give you an example that some of you may have read about in *Forbes* or the *New York Times*. Two marketing guys at Target Stores challenged Andrew Pole, a statistician, to figure out if a customer was pregnant even if she didn't want them to know. The marketers explained that new parents are the holy grail in retail. As many of you know, new parents don't have time to shop, and instead of buying groceries at Publix and screwdrivers at Lowe's, they tend to buy everything at one store if it has it, which Target does. If Target could identify new parents early and get them buying everything at Target, it would have a huge lifetime value. When the baby is born, they will need a crib and all the baby items. Then, the kid goes to school, and they need clothes and school supplies. But the marketers knew that they couldn't just use birth records, which are public record, because everyone can do that. They wanted to know earlier than everyone else. They wanted to send advertisements to moms-to-be in their second trimester, which is when they start buying prenatal vitamins and maternity clothes."

"Target had been capturing guest data for years, so Andrew Pole decided he was up for the challenge. He started with the historical buying data of women who had signed up for Target's baby registries in the past and began testing the data. His team discovered patterns such as the fact that pregnant women switch to unscented soaps and lotions. The team at Target looked at changes in the buying patterns and, ultimately, the data revealed about 25 products that, when analyzed together, gave them a pregnancy prediction score. This score allowed them to predict the delivery date so Target could send coupons at various stages of the pregnancy."

"Now, allegedly, Mr. Pole and his team were a little too good at this. The story was that a dad in Minnesota got the mail and discovered Target was sending his teenage daughter coupons for baby clothes and cribs. The dad went to Target and complained to the manager that they were trying to get his daughter pregnant. The manager apologized and said he would look into it. A few days later when the manager called the man, the man informed him that his daughter was pregnant. So, Target knew before the family did. I know that is borderline creepy. I am sure Target now hides the creepiness by including coupons for lawn mowers too," Ally laughed. I looked around the room, and the faces looked a little shocked. "Do you think that's creepy?"

"Yes but pretty amazing too," said Steve.

"Think of the power of that insight! As you brainstorm, ask yourself what data would you want to know about your clients, about geographic areas... What if you could predict natural disasters and ship more essentials, like water, first aid, and clean-up supplies to those areas in advance? Let your mind wander!"

"Let's work on an example of what we are looking for together. The questions I want to ask my crystal ball are 'what products are the most profitable, and which clients are more likely to purchase these products?' At the top of a sticky note, I write the question. Then, I write why I want the answer. I want to provide the sales team with a list of clients most likely to purchase more of the most profitable items to increase profits. Then, I write what action would be taken when the end user has the data. Salespeople will promote the most profitable items to clients who are likely to buy high-margin items. Finally, I want to note the effect and economic outcome. Note that it's okay to be wrong. Give it your best estimate. I would write on my note something like this: 'We could increase profits by $750,000 a year, also resulting in higher commissions to the salespeople.'"

"Does this make sense? It doesn't have to be perfect; it's just a start. If you have ideas that you came up with earlier, please put those on the large sticky notes too. So, for each idea, you will write:

- The question being asked
- Why you're asking it
- What actions will be taken
- The economic effect.

You will have 20 minutes for this, and I'll play a little music for you. Any questions?"

"What if there is no economic effect but another effect like increased employee satisfaction?" a young woman with long dark hair asked.

"Employee satisfaction leads to fewer people leaving and, therefore, less recruiting cost, so it does have an economic effect," said John from HR.

"Oh, I get it. I just have to keep going to get to the economic effect," said the young woman.

"Yes, almost everything will directly or indirectly have an economic effect. Any other questions?" Ally scanned the room. "Start now!" Ally hit "play" on her iPhone.

I began writing feverishly. Pulling out my notebook, I jotted down my earlier ideas and added the why and an economic impact. This process was so simple. I loved that everyone in the room could do it. By having a mix of people from different functional areas, we were bound to have ideas that impacted all aspects of our business. When Ally made the call for five minutes remaining, I glanced around the room. Everyone was writing with their heads down. Some were rubbing their hands to alleviate the cramping. The sensation of pride overcame me. This was my team.

"Okay, stop," said Ally as she stopped the music. "Now, we are going to get in teams. The teams must self-form, so look around. Who do you want on your team? There are a couple rules. You must have one person from each functional area, so there's a minimum of one HR, one marketing, one finance, one operations, and one IT person on each team. No team may be more than seven people. No team can have more than one executive on the team. Once you form your team, you will want to choose a facilitator. The facilitator will help guide the process and is responsible for keeping the team on track in the allotted time. Any questions?" Ally scanned the room. "Then form your teams."

At first, it looked like chaos. Some people were clearly trying to get on a team with a particular person. A few had the look of schoolchildren hoping to be chosen on a team. As the teams started to form, there was a little trading going on.

A woman with short brown hair shouted, "We need a marketing person, please."

That was followed by a tall, thin man crying out, "Any extra IT?" which prompted a short, stocky young man I presumed to be from IT to respond, "Phil, I'll join your team."

The teams somehow managed to find one person from each functional area without any guidance from Ally. When it was done, everyone seemed happy to have a group. My group had seven people of diverse ages. "This will be interesting," I thought.

"Before you start reviewing and prioritizing your ideas, make sure you select your facilitator. His or her job is to keep you moving so that you get through all the ideas and rank them. This person is not the leader but just the facilitator. So, he or she doesn't get the final say. On your team, the chain of command that you are accustomed to no longer exists. So, I am sorry, James, but you are just another team member and not the boss," Ally said, placing a hand on my shoulder.

"In fact, if an executive is on your team, that person is not allowed to be the facilitator. Each of you brings a unique knowledge, experience, and insight. Leverage it. You may also discover the millennials on your team may have a very different perspective than the Generation Xers. I believe when we combine the generations and different backgrounds, we prime the pump for innovative ideas. Crazy ideas are celebrated! Before you start, you will want to create a team name. Come up with a name that reflects your team, but don't waste too much time on it. Just remember to keep it clean; HR is here," Ally laughed.

"Once you have your team name, write it at the top of your flip chart. Then, the facilitators will have each person read their ideas and place them on the flip chart. If the group comes up with new ideas during the process, that's fine. Write them down. Once all the ideas are shared, each person will receive three stickers to vote. Remember, green is for the best idea. After the initial voting is complete, the facilitator will guide the team to select the top three ideas. The team will then present their three ideas to the entire group. Your presenter does not have to be the facilitator, so you can choose someone else to present. However, executives are not allowed to present. Any questions?"

"How much time do we have?" shouted out a sharply dressed man of Asian descent in the back.

"Oh, yes. Sorry, since this is your first time, and I see you guys have a lot of ideas, we will give you one hour and 15 minutes. But before we start, we will give you 10 minutes to get some water and take a break."

It was interesting sitting back and just being a team player on the Data Ninjas. Initially, I found it hard not to share my thoughts, but I then realized my team was very creative without me. A couple times, I started to dominate the conversation. However, Betsy, the facilitator, an older woman from finance, stepped in and politely reminded me to let others finish their thoughts, which made me laugh. As people were sharing ideas, I noticed several people would start to scribble down additional ideas. It took us about 30 minutes just to read all the ideas. Then, Betsy had us vote by walking up to the flip chart and casting our sticker votes. When we were done, there were five ideas that clearly had more stickers than the rest.

"Is everyone in agreement that we just focus on discussing these five ideas and decide which three we present?" asked Betsy. We all nodded in agreement. "Great, I'll read each one out loud so we all know the five contenders, and then, let's discuss each one. I think we should explore the why and the economic effect of each in more detail. Does that work?"

"Yes, but could we also look at feasibility," said Amit from IT. "If I am not mistaken, our goal is to present three ideas that could deliver a minimal viable product within 90 days and prove that the concept works. The pilot or MacGyver test will help determine the real economic impact." Just then, Ally walked by and overheard. She smiled a big sassy smile at Amit, confirming that he was correct.

"You are right. Great reminder, Amit," said Betsy, clearly very proud of her facilitator role that she was elected to. "Okay, I will read the five. Jot down notes if you like, but no discussion until all are read. Since we only have 30 minutes, we need to really focus our time." The team nodded.

Once we narrowed the list down to the three winners, Betsy grabbed a marker and wrote each idea on the top of a clean flip chart page. She then documented our ideas on why, the economic impact, and the feasibility. With Amit's help, we even discussed how we collect the data in a data mart.

When the hour was up, we were feeling confident with our ideas. Ally had each group present their top three ideas. I was floored by some of the creative ideas. In order to expedite things, Ally gave each group three stickers, and they were to vote as a team for the top three ideas. Once again, it became apparent which ones were preferred.

"Well, we are down to six amazing, game-changing ideas! You guys should be so proud! Imagine what would happen to the bottom line if all six of these were implemented? You do realize that, eventually, we will implement all of them, right?" Ally's smile sparkled.

"Each team will do a deeper analysis on two of the six ideas and will share their thoughts. You can leverage what you have already heard about each idea and create your own thoughts. Ultimately, we will need to choose one idea that we MacGyver. The ideas not chosen now will simply become our backlog, and we will get to them later. As you analyze the two ideas, I want you to calculate the economic value of the idea over one and five years, create a feasibility analysis and, finally, identify what skills or knowledge the team that delivers this will need."

"Once we identify which idea to MacGyver, we will then create the special forces team to deliver it based on the skills the project will require. You will be able to make recommendations on the skills and knowledge needed for the particular initiative. We will then ask for volunteers that think they have the most to contribute to the team. I know all of you want to be on the initial team, but it's like football. The quarterback is not on the field when the other team has the ball because his skills are not needed. Don't worry, you will all get your turn."

"One rule: if your team created the idea, you cannot do a deep analysis on your own idea. You must analyze another team's ideas. Any questions?" Ally allocated each team two ideas and set the timer for 60 minutes.

"Can you explain the feasibility analysis? I am a little confused," stated someone in the back of the room.

"Sure, you want to look at do you have the data, will the users use the solution.. You know the simplest way to flush out potential issues is to ask each team member what their biggest concern is with regard to the project. Since the team members come from different functional areas, you should get a good understanding of the potential issues and develop a feasibility analysis. Remember there are no wrong answers," said Ally.

"What a great idea," I thought. She's soliciting multiple points of view on each idea by having us analyze it. By working on other people's ideas, we now believe in them because we have skin in the game. I realized much of what Ally was doing was building internal support for the idea while developing collaboration and teamwork. This was what Ally was talking about when she said engagement was the secret to increasing end user adoption. How simple. Get them to have skin in the game. I jotted the idea down in my notebook.

Once the analysis was done and each team presented, the six ideas were easily narrowed to two top contenders. Ally facilitated the discussion in which every team shared their thoughts on the top contenders.

The first idea covered our fleet of trucks and predictive maintenance. How could we know which trucks were likely to break down before they do? Knowing this would allow us to fix the trucks prior to the breakdown. The foreseeable results included lack of spoilage of goods, increased on-time deliveries, which would increase customer loyalty, and less attrition due to drivers of broken-down trucks being stressed and losing commissions.

The team felt this data and the resulting actions could increase market share. Our competitors' fleets were as old as ours, and they would still break down and be less reliable. It was anticipated that repair costs would decrease because when parts break, it causes other issues and often costs a lot more to repair than replacing the part in advance. Additionally, we would not have to tow the trucks for service. The team felt that we had the data and could begin seeing positive results within the 90-day rollout. Ally titled this idea "the fleet predictive maintenance."

The second idea dealt with the profitability of a client location for each delivery. Currently, we struggle to calculate the profitability of each client and did not have any visibility to location profitability. We have visibility to profit margin by product sold. The idea that we may have been selling to clients and locations that were not profitable was something intriguing. By looking at the data related to the client's order volume by delivery, the products they ordered, and the profit on those products, we could gain increased visibility to delivery profitability. From this, we could identify client locations that are less profitable and may discover that we need to develop new minimum order quantities or provide recommended bundles to increase the order. We could offer discounts on higher profit margin items to optimize the customer orders based on their previous purchases. My mind was spinning. This could be massive.

"The question is: what is the profitability of each delivery the driver makes to each location?" stated Ally. "Let's discuss the why."

All the teams displayed an excitement. This could massively impact the bottom line. I started running numbers in my head. If we could cut out deliveries to the customers that were not profitable by using predictive data to guide our salespeople to recommend better product offerings tailored to the client or provide the client with a discount for a certain level of order that was based on profit instead of volume, that could be huge. I listened as the analysis flooded from the teams. "Why hadn't we done this years ago?" I thought. By requiring the team to be mixed, it fostered a completely different experience, as ideas came from all points of view. Every now and then, the team started going down the rabbit hole, and Ally would masterfully ask a question that moved the conversation forward. This process would have taken us months without a skilled facilitator and the *Business Intelligence Bull's-eye Framework*. What was amazing was that everyone was on board. There was no saying why it couldn't be done, but there were creative solutions for how to make it happen.

"Well, I think I know the answer based on the team's engagement and discussion, but let's take a vote. How many of you think we should start with the fleet predictive maintenance idea as our first MacGyver program? Please raise your hands high." Two hands raised. "And how many of you vote for the customer location delivery profitability idea?" Almost all the hands went up. Ally applauded. "Congratulations, everyone! Now, of course, this is subject to executive veto, so I will ask the executive team if there is any reservation you have in having the team execute this initiative?"

I shook my head and said, "No, I think this is fabulous! Let's do it."

"Yes."

"I agree." The others were all nodding their heads.

"Great, then the next step is to identify the special forces team members that we need. We need to start with the skills and knowledge the team will need to succeed. Then, we will take volunteers for the team." Ally facilitated a discussion of what knowledge and skills the team would need.

"Well, I think what you have outlined is fabulous. You have included someone that knows your data, subject matter experts from sales and operations, as well as someone with finance knowledge on how it will impact the bottom line. You have accomplished so much today. You guys are awesome. The next step will be forming the team, so when we conclude, if you think you have knowledge and experience that the team needs and you are interested in being considered for this initial project, please provide me your name during the break."

"Once everyone interested is on the list, the executives with the help of the managers will evaluate and select the players for our first team. But remember, if you don't get selected initially, we may still need your help along the way, and there will be many more opportunities. The executives have committed to transformation and, as you can see by this room, there are many more projects to come. We just want to start with one, prove the methodology, and then do another one. It's not uncommon for companies that master the process to have multiple projects going simultaneously. Are there any questions?" asked Ally.

Amit raised his hand. "I am excited that we have everyone focusing on the same thing. That will make a huge difference compared to how we did things in the past. But I am still confused about how we will accomplish this. It's clear to me that we will need to build a specific data mart to get the data the way we need it; however, currently, we do not have predictive software and don't have anyone with predictive analytic software skills to my knowledge."

"Oh, Amit, is that analytical brain of yours building the models and processes in your head?" Ally asked in a playful way. "You are on the right track. We don't have all the factors defined yet. Once we select the team, the team will begin the official *Business Analytics Agile Methodology*, or as we call it, *BAAM*, which is a Scrum method we will use. Like we discussed yesterday, with *BAAM*, the team is responsible for delivering value to the business. The team works together on shared goals. Once the team members have the goal, it's up to them to figure out how to do the work, who does the work, what software and tools are needed, to identify roadblocks and impediments, resolve scope issues, and work with non-team members when needed. The team's goal is a minimum viable product that could be as simple as a dashboard. Later, it could be more complex with bells and whistles. The team will deliver a working product after each sprint. Every sprint, the team improves the delivered product a little bit, but each time, it must be something useable. The team will have a product owner whose job it is to collaborate with stakeholders to inspect and adapt the product vision to make it as valuable as possible. The team will create user stories that define the functionality from the user's perspective."

"User stories?" Amit asked with an inquisitive look.

"Yes. Here's an example of a user story. As a salesperson, I want to see the forecasted profit on a specific client's order so I can offer the customer additional items of interest and make the delivery profitable. Basically, it is defining the user's need and why. The team will create many user stories and then determine which to include in the first sprint. Items not selected for the first sprint, which is usually four to six weeks long, will be added to a backlog. The team will learn as it goes. When the team discovers something, the team members may add new items to the backlog of functionality that were not included in the first sprint. It's about continuous improvement and constant response to changes. The team members will use feedback loops that will allow them to constantly inspect and adjust so the product delivers maximum value instead of building the whole solution and then having users test it. The team will have short standup meetings every morning where team members will say what they worked on yesterday, what they are working on today, and what hurdles they anticipate. A Scrum master will be responsible for helping remove the hurdles."

"Just having regular meetings would help eliminate confusion," said Amit.

"Yes, that's the idea: to eliminate miscommunication and get everyone moving in the same direction. But to get back to your question, during the planning stages, the team members will determine if they have the right tools or what they are missing. A hurdle might be that Fairplay Distributing does not have predictive software, so the Scrum master will be responsible for helping to solve that issue."

"In my experience, when the team first identifies what the solution needs to solve and provide through the user stories, the team members are in a much better place to select software. User stories define what functionality you must have in the software. When you work with the various software vendors, you will be able to communicate exactly what you need, resulting in a very efficient selection process. It's always frustrating when I work with a client who has not defined what success looks like but buys new software based on features and functionality. I know you guys have some BI software, and that's great. We always start with what you have and see if it meets your needs. If it's determined that you need to supplement your current software, the team will provide details to IT, which will help with selecting software. It's amazing how many companies start the software selection process and never complete a detailed requirements discovery process. Congratulations, you guys have already started one."

"How have we started?" Amit asked with a puzzled look on his face.

Ally flipped her hair and beamed at Amit. "Well, you have been doing it all day. The room is full of ideas about what you want to do with business intelligence and predictive software. Even the runner-up idea defines functionality you want the software to handle, right? You've defined that you need a tool that can handle predictive maintenance and customer analytics."

I glanced around the room, and a light bulb went on. We have a lot of software requirements defined, and the end user requirements were all over the flip charts. "Most clients take all this amazing information and have IT add systems and infrastructure requirements, like integration with SQL. Before you know it, you have a list for the software salespeople to show you."

"Wow," Bob said. "That solves a big hurdle. When we are tasked with selecting software, most of the time, we don't have a good understanding of what the end users really want. No offense, guys, but in the past, most users are too busy to really share their vision and requirements, so we make assumptions as to what you need."

"Yes, that's common. Have you ever bought software that you later realized does not meet your long-term needs?" Ally asked.

"A few times," Bob admitted.

"I think you probably have about... what? Five to seven years of ideas here?" Ally waved her hands in the air, gesturing to all the flip charts. "Since we have already identified that we probably will need some additional software, I anticipate that we will need another team. This one will collaborate with the first team on requirements but will run the software selection process."

"So, Amit, does that make sense to you?"

"Absolutely!" he said, smiling like he discovered a secret.

"Any other questions?" The room was buzzing with excitement. "Okay, thank you guys for playing all out! And that completes our initial sessions," Ally said, clapping. The entire room clapped, and a couple of the executives even stood up to give the entire group a standing ovation.

Key Takeaways:

- Mixing teams to have members from various departments provides the teams with various perspectives.

- Designate facilitators for groups and meetings to keep the flow.

- When evaluating ideas, colored stickers can be used to vote to quickly focus the team on the top ideas.

- The minimal viable product (MVP) is a solution that has basic functionality. It is a like a pilot to prove if the idea delivers the expected value.

- Getting everyone's thoughts allows for them to have skin in the game and helps with end user adoption.

- Agile and Scrum methods like the *Business Analytics Agile Methodology (BAAM)* leverages users' stories that describe how the users will interact with the solution.

- The brainstorming sessions in the *Business Intelligence Bull's-eye Framework* create a backlog of ideas so the team can continue to deliver solutions that positively impact the bottom line.

Are you ready to have some fun brainstorming crazy ideas? Crazy ideas lead to innovation. You are making fantastic progress by reading this book. Keep it up. If you haven't signed up for the bonus material, I strongly encourage you to do it now.

Simply register at www.Heatherized.com/bookbonus, and you will gain access to many tools to aid you in your journey to become an analytic leader!

Here is what you'll receive:

- BI Action Assessment Indicator
- Core Values worksheet
- Questionnaires
- Sample job description for attracting BI superstars
- Videos to improve communication and provide time-saving methods
- And more!

Sign up today at www.Heatherized.com/BookBonus.

CHAPTER 8

Lessons Learned

"Be the change you want to see in the world."

–Mahatma Gandhi

Several weeks later, Ally arrived in the office wearing a dark green dress that highlighted her green eyes. As she walked into my office, I jumped up to give her a hug.

"How was your trip?" she asked.

"Fabulous, thanks for asking. How's MacGyver going?" I asked anxiously.

"I am sure you already have heard the gossip," she winked. "But the team is working hard. We have taken over the Chicago room as our war room. You should see it—sticky notes everywhere! We have a Scrum board that has the backlog. The team has identified phase one and is really embracing the *BAAM* process. Today, we are teaching them how to facilitate a dashboard design workshop with end users. Our technique helps them hit a home run the first time because we have the end users draw pictures of what they would like. Tomorrow, they get to learn presentation skills. That's always a fun day."

"I hope the end users draw better than me," I smiled. "You know, I was talking to Bob yesterday, and he said that he's seen a big difference in his IT team. He said one guy that did not make the special forces for this project came to him and mentioned that he would like to get his Scrum Master certification so he's ready for the next mission. Bob mentioned they feel valued and respected more."

"That doesn't surprise me. IT gets a bad rap in a lot of organizations, and they really should be a key part of transformation. So, James, I am curious. What did you think of the first phase of the *Business Intelligence Bull's-eye Framework?*"

"If I put a number to it, I would score it a 10, and my word? Hmm... 'amazing.' No, maybe 'life-changing.' Wait, is that two words?" We both laughed. "Seriously, I realize we still have a lot of work, but just the initial phase changed people's attitudes. They are engaging one another, and they are trying to speak the same language. It's crazy. I don't really understand how." I paused.

"It really is quite simple," Ally said. "It's hope and a common goal. Teams jell together when they all have a common goal that they defined and know they are in it together. They feel valued. They have a voice."

"And, apparently, they have some really good ideas." I smiled.

"Yes, when asked, they do have good ideas. What key takeaways did you get from the first part of the process?"

"Key takeaways? You mean, besides the fact we were doing it all wrong? I guess we were being reactive instead of proactive. The biggest lesson I learned is that business intelligence involves people, processes, tools, and data, but the people part is the most important. Without people having a common understanding of the goal and effective methods of communication, you don't get anywhere."

"Exactly."

"You know, I was in San Francisco last week, and they were having a dragon boat race. Have you ever seen one?"

"Yes, they have those here in Tampa on the Hillsborough river. They're the long boats where they have paddles on each side and person hitting a drum to create the cadence for the paddlers. I would want to be the drummer," Ally said.

"They also have a person in the back steering. But I watched them, and I saw this one team. Oh my, they were bad. They were completely out of sync. They had all the strong people on one side, so they kept turning. It was as if the two sides of the boat were at war with each other. Clearly, they had not practiced. But as I sat there watching them, I realized that's how we were delivering our BI before. We weren't in sync. Heck, we didn't even know where the finish line was. But there was another boat where everyone was timed perfectly. The drummer was communicating the stroke pace, and everyone followed perfectly. They were a machine, flying through the water like a missile. They made the bad team look like they were standing still. That's how I want our team to perform. And thanks to you, I think we are getting there."

"I love that analogy. So, what do you think went well?"

"What went well? Hmm, I think how the concepts were taught was great. By using games, I believe people were more open to learning and not afraid of looking ignorant. I know when you had Mark throw darts at the bull's-eye, that really hit home for me. It was definitely an 'aha' moment. I also loved the sticky note process and time blocking. Everyone's ideas were heard and yet, we filtered to the important stuff quickly."

"I see you have incorporated it into your life," Ally said, pointing to my office wall covered in sticky notes.

"Yes, it's amazing how it keeps me focused on what's really important. You know, I actually copied all my notes in this." I turned and grabbed the gray journal from the corner of my desk. On the cover of the notebook was written "BE THE CHANGE YOU WANT TO SEE IN THE WORLD" in yellow letters. "Mary, my wife, gave me this, and I love it."

"I am jealous. That's a cool journal. And I am proud of you for reviewing your notes. I find that just flipping through old notes from training programs helps me get back on track when I start slipping into bad habits. Any ideas about what we could have done better?"

"Wow, that is hard. Maybe we could have had an all-company meeting to discuss the change and what's going on for everyone. I think maybe there were people who were not invited to the foundations day that were feeling left out and were concerned."

"That's a great point. Some companies are a little reluctant to do that until they understand and experience the initial round of the *Business Intelligence Bull's-eye Framework*. It's kind of like when you first start dating someone, you don't introduce them to your family until you know it works," Ally smiled. "If you don't mind, James, before I go meet with the team, I would like you to take a couple minutes and complete the BI Action Assessment Indicator again. It will be fun to see where you are now."

Ally handed me a printed version of the form. I read the first questions out loud. "One: Our executives not only support our BI initiatives, but they clearly and regularly communicate the strategic goals of the organization. Well, I would say we are now at a nine."

"Do you remember how you scored it initially?" asked Ally, pulling out my prior form.

"I think a two."

"Nope," she smiled. "A one. You've come a long way, baby," Ally laughed.

As I read through the rest of the form, I was amazed how far we had come. However, there was still a lot of work to get us to where we were going.

———————

In the following months, the special forces team built a data mart to store the data needed to provide the salespeople with visibility of the profit margin by product. The predictive analytics component to determine which clients were most likely to buy the higher profit items was put to the backlog. The team discovered that by simply having the profit margin of the products and knowing which clients had purchased those products in the past, they could provide the sales reps with information that helped them in their sales presentations. The sales reps were able to pull up a dashboard on their iPads that included the customers' purchases and a filter to see the recommended items. We know there's a lot of room for improvement, but just rolling out the minimal viable product was a huge win. Now, the sales team is sharing ideas about how to make it better. With each sprint, they receive better tools. The results are starting to show up on our bottom line.

Ally gave us the art of facilitation, and we are seeing a ripple effect across the organization. Meetings are productive, people are present, and we spend less time in meetings.

The IT team has started a special forces team of their own to deal with the data issue. They collaborate with the BI team and have indexed and optimized existing data marts while designing a data delivery roadmap. The goal is to get the data in a format that the BI team can use to deploy self-service soon.

Quarterly, we have Ally come in and facilitate a review of where we are. We evaluate our BI roadmap and build on it. We discuss what has changed in the business and confirm and communicate our strategic goals and priorities. Ally also oversees quarterly meetings with end users to discover any new requirements and communicate any new plans. The meetings energize the team and makes everyone feel like they are a part of the transformation.

We are defining a timeline to add the components of the continuous loop solutions. Finance is looking to work with the BI team and integrate the budget and forecasting processes later this year.

If you asked me what's the biggest lesson I learned, I would say it was to not to wait. Don't sit on the fence and expect IT to deliver. Executives need to be actively engaged in business intelligence. They need to take the time to learn and lead their organization through the data revolution. If you don't act now, your competitors will! What do you want your legacy to be?

You rock! You are officially more advanced in analytic leadership than the majority of your peers. You are on the road to transform your company with data and analytics. I am very proud of you. If you didn't register for the supplemental materials yet, you should do it now and complete the BI Action Assessment Indicator.

Simply register at www.Heatherized.com/bookbonus, and you will gain access to many tools to aid you in your journey to become an analytic leader!

Here is what you'll receive:

- BI Action Assessment Indicator
- Core Values worksheet
- Questionnaires
- Sample job description for attracting BI superstars
- Videos to improve communication and provide time-saving methods
- And more!

Sign up today at www.Heatherized.com/BookBonus.

Let's Continue Working Together

Ready to Take Action and Become an Analytic Leader?

When is now a good time to act? It's your time to raise your value and learn to lead your organization through the data revolution. Gain the skills to empower the nerds so they can connect with the business and increase end user adoption of your business intelligence solutions. Create an environment where people love to learn and are willing to try new, innovative ideas. Not only do you get the tools and frameworks to empower your team and become an analytic leader, you will also learn the mindset and core values it takes to transform your company like James Brown in this book. Now is time to conquer your market. If you don't take the first step, your competition might. Visit www.Heatherized.com/bookbonus for tools to get started. If you want to expedite the process, bring Heather into you organization to show you the way at www.heatherized.com/hire-heather/.

Other Programs and Offerings by Heatherized:

Analytic Leadership Executive Program – Learn to lead your organization through the data revolution. Includes:

- How to rapidly define your analytics roadmap
- How to transition the company to embrace data
- Communicating the vision
- How to find the right team members
- Dealing with millennials
- And more

Business Intelligence Bull's-eye Framework – Experience coaching with Heather to realize quick business intelligence wins that grow your bottom line.

Destination Dashboard – This program teaches business analytics and business intelligence professionals how to partner with the business to deliver dashboards users love.

Software Selection Process Framework – This program teaches IT professionals how to run an effective software selection process. It's designed for business intelligence software, but the framework works for all software. It includes negotiation skills, scorecards, and requirements definitions.

Rapid Requirements Discovery Program – This program teaches you the art of getting end users to define and communicate what technology can do for them and increases end user adoption. This can significantly decrease project costs.

Software Presentation Skills – This coaching program teaches you the art of software presentation. Heather will coach attendees on increasing end user adoption and software demonstration. It's great for business analysts, IT, and software pre-sales people.

Value Added Reseller Mastermind Group – Are you a software VAR that wants to grow your business and reduce your risk? This program was created based on requests by Heather's competitors. They often sought her insight on legal structures, sales tax, hiring talent, exit strategies, and more. This is designed for principals of VARs.

Executive Analytic Leaders Mastermind Group – This is a mastermind group designed for executives who have transformed into analytic leaders and want to network and share ideas with other like-minded people. This program is software-agnostic, so we don't care what tools you use. This is an invite-only group, but if you would like to be considered, email hcole@heatherized.com.

IT Soft Skills Training - This is a customizable program designed to increase communication and connections between IT and the business.

For more information on these programs, visit www.heatherized .com or contact me at hcole@heatherized.com.

About the Author

Heather L. Cole transforms executives into analytic leaders so they can guide their organizations through the cultural shift required to become data and analytics- driven. Companies that adapt quickly to the data revolution will conquer their markets and lead innovation in their industries.

Heather's entertaining and informative speeches, workshops, blogs, and executive advisory services provide clients with pragmatic methods they can implement immediately to deliver "Faster, Cheaper Analytics."

Her *Business Intelligence Bull's-eye Framework* is designed to help companies identify quick wins with business intelligence and guide companies to save millions of dollars in recurring revenue.

Heather is the founder of Lodestar Solutions and Heatherized, Inc. As an Executive Business Analytics Advisor, Heather provides a diverse knowledge in Finance, IT, Law, Psychology, Sales, and Marketing. Heather is a Certified High-Performance Coach, licensed attorney, Scrum Master, and has over 25 years of experience in business intelligence. She is also a bestselling author.

Heather is a five-time winner of the IBM Information Champion Award for being a thought leader in analytics and is on the board of the Tampa Bay chapter of FEI (Financial Executives International).

Heather is also on the board of Ready for Life, a nonprofit that helps young adults who age out of foster care.

Heather is originally from the western suburbs of Chicago and now lives in Tampa, Florida, and Breckenridge, Colorado, with her English creme golden retriever, Ozzie. When she's not at conferences learning new methods, Heather trail runs, skis, reads, enjoys nature rafting, and watching hockey.

For more information on Heather L. Cole, go to www.heatherized. com. You can follow her on Twitter @Heatherize and connect with her on LinkedIn at www.linkedin.com/in/heatherlcole/.

Book Heather L. Cole to Speak

Book Heather L. Cole as your keynote speaker, and you're guaranteed to make your event inspirational, motivational, highly entertaining, and unforgettable! For over two decades, Heather L. Cole has been educating, entertaining, motivating, and inspiring executives and professionals who want to make a difference in their organizations by leveraging technology and data. Her story includes growing up in her parent's software company that provided data and analytics information on the futures markets in the early 80s.

As a teenager working for her parents, Heather discovered that many people fear technology and created her own methods to increase end users' success and transform people and organizations. She also realized that how technology-savvy and highly analytical people— the nerds—communicate does not translate to the masses. Over the years, she learned the art of translating highly technical concepts to normal people. As a result, she calls herself a *socialized nerd.* But it was her discovery of Tony Robbins and his ability to help people make massive changes in their lives by using a repeatable framework that changed her life forever. Heather is determined to become the Tony Robbins of data and analytics.

Her unique style inspires, empowers, and entertains audiences while giving them the tools and strategies they need to succeed in the data revolution. For more info and to book Heather for your next event, visit http://heatherized.com/hire-heather/.

Acknowledgements

The original edition of this book was written, edited, and published in one month, but it is built on 25+ years of mistakes, and the support of dedicated team members and wonderful clients who provided inspiration and success stories from the field. I'm so grateful for the support and patience you've given me.

Susan Cole, my mom, you always told me to "make the world a little bit better." You insisted that I must always "challenge" myself. Well, we both know that didn't always work out as planned, but it resulted in a lot of "learning experiences" that made me who I am today. Thanks for always being my cheerleader.

Wesley Cole, my dad, you started me down the data and analytics road before I could even drive. The Turbo Pascal books you gave me for my sixteenth birthday were the envy of all my friends. Not everyone can say they traveled the country training futures traders how to use PCs with software that provide analytics on pork bellies and gold. Who ever thought that my first job working for your companies, Quantitative Management and Applied Decision Systems (both horribly named), would lead me to writing a book on data and analytics? You have always been my inspiration to socialize the nerds. You've come a long way.

Mr. Marc Gilbert, my fifth-grade teacher at Wildrose Elementary in St. Charles, Illinois, I will never be able to tell you this personally, but there is not a day that goes by that I don't think about you.

There's a saying: "Every now and then, someone comes into your life and changes everything!" You were the one. I just wish I could tell your family how you changed my world! You are definitely my angel.

Ms. Bernardi, my freshman English teacher, as much as I despised you in high school, you were correct. I was gifted in math and science and not in English.

Finally, to my wonderful customers and clients: you're my inspiration and mission! It's an honor and a privilege to serve and support you.

Heather L. Cole
Tampa, Florida, and Breckenridge, Colorado

Endnotes

1. "Artificial Intelligence is Positioned to be Game-changer." *60 Minutes*. Charlie Rose. CBS, 25 June 2017. Television.

2. Rohaidi, Nurfilzah. "IBM's Watson Detected Rare Leukemia In Just 10 Minutes." *Asian Scientist Magazine*, 15 Aug. 2016, www.asianscientist.com/2016/08/topnews/ibm-watson-rare-leukemia-university-tokyo-artificial-intelligence/.

3. Siegel, Eric. *Predictive Analytics: The Power to Predict Who Will Click, Buy, Lie, or Die.* Hoboken, NJ: John Wiley & Sons, Inc., 2013. Print.

4. Gartner, Inc. (2017, January 16)."Gartner Says More Than 40 Percent of Data Science Tasks Will Be Automated by 2020," 16 Jan. 2017. Press release, www.gartner.com/newsroom/id/3570917

5. Sutherland, Jeff & Sutherland, JJ. *Scrum: The Art of Doing Twice the Work in Half the Time.* New York: Random House LLC, 2014. Print.

6. Eissler, Annie. "Top KPIs that Every Distributor Should be Tracking." MITS, 9 Jan. 2017, mits.com/blog/top-kpis-every-distributor-should-be-tracking

83973077R00083

Made in the USA
Lexington, KY
17 March 2018